S0-BOB-469

DRESSING RIGHT

DRESSING RIGHT

A GUIDE FOR MEN

CHARLES HIX

WITH BRIAN BURDINE

Photography by
HANK KEMME
MICHAEL O'BRIEN
BRUCE WEBER
HERB RITTS
CHRIS MEAD
LOÍC RAOUT
PALMA KOLANSKY

Drawings by
JOEL NAPRSTEK

ST. MARTIN'S PRESS
New York

PHOTOGRAPHS

HANK KEMME

P. 25 *lower right*; 29 *right*; 59 *lower right*; 60 *lower right*; 74 *top left*; 80; 84 *left*; 87; 109-110; 113; 119; 123-124; 127 *left*; 131; 140 *left*; 149; 152; 155-159; 165 *top left*; 170; 173; 176; 182; 183 *right*; 185; 189; 193 *left*; 195; 196 *top*; 197 *left, top right*; 198 *left, lower right*; 200 *right*; 201 *lower left, right*; 202 *left*; 203 *right*; 206 *right*; 208 *right*; 212 *left*; 213 *right*; 214; 226 *right*; 228-230; 231 *top*; 232; 233 *lower right*; 234 *right*; 238 *top left*.

PALMA KOLANSKY

P. 32; 48; 66 *bottom*; 85; 167 *left*; 199; 210; 233 *left*.

CHRIS MEAD

P. 25 *lower left*; 44; 68-69; 71; 84 *right*; 88-97; 135-138; 145-147; 175; 212 *right*; 238 *lower left, right*.

MICHAEL O'BRIEN

P. 25 *top*; 28 *top*; 46; 57; 59 *top*; 60 *lower left*; 64; 67; 72 *left, lower right*; 74 *lower left, top right*; 75; 79; 81-82; 98-99; 102; 106; 112; 120-121; 128 *right*; 140 *lower right*; 141 *top*; 148; 151; 153-154; 161; 163-164; 167 *lower right*; 168 *left*; 169; 178-179; 183 *left*; 193 *right*; 196 *bottom*; 198 *top right*; 200 *left*; 204; 208 *lower left*; 211; 226 *left*; 227; 234 *left*; 236; 239; 243.

LOÍC RAOUT

P. 29 *lower left*; 65; 126 *upper left, upper right*; 132; 201 *top left*; 209; 216; 237.

HERB RITTS

P. 43; 47; 49; 53; 63; 66 *top*; 100-101; 107-108; 111; 115-117; 118 *top left, top right, lower right*; 122; 126 *lower left*; 127 *right*; 160; 165 *lower right*; 166; 167 *top right*; 181; 197 *lower right*; 203 *left*; 207; 208 *top left*; 215; 240-241.

BRUCE WEBER

Cover & all color photographs. P. 12-15; 28 *bottom*; 29 *top left*; 41; 51; 55; 59 *lower left*; 60 *top*; 70; 72 *top right*; 74 *lower right*; 105; 114; 118 *lower left*; 126 *lower right*; 128 *left*; 129-130; 133; 140 *top right*; 141 *bottom*; 165 *lower left, top right*; 168 *right*; 171; 202 *right*; 205; 206 *left*; 213 *left*; 225; 231 *bottom*; 233 *top right*; 235; 242.

DRESSING RIGHT

Copyright © by Charles Hix, 1978. Drawings copyright © by Joel Naprstek, 1978.

Library of Congress Cataloging in Publication Data

Hix, Charles.
  Dressing right.

  Includes index.
  1. Men's clothing. 2. Grooming for men.
I. Burdine, Brian, joint author. II. Title.
TT618.H58   646'.32   78-3972
ISBN 0-312-21968-7 cloth
ISBN 0-312-21969-5 paper

To
my sister Pat
who taught me to care;
my parents
who supplied me with sweaters and love;
my friends in the menswear industry
Alan, Alex & Lynn, Arnie, Barbara, Bert, Bill, Bob,
Chip, Douglas, George, Gil & Joanna, Jack, Jeff, John,
Lee, Luciano, Paul, Roberta, Ronald, Sal & Nancy
and the scores more
who helped with the myriad pieces (Deborah, too);
the photographers
who improved my vision;
the models
who fleshed out the ideas and
without whom the book couldn't be;
Vicki Pribble
who did it out of kindness (Zoli as well);
Michael Taylor
who was survival during the monsoon;
Brian Burdine
who filled the maroon ashtray with butts
and his eyes with drops
while suffering and dreaming with me;
Michael Denneny
who made it all happen;
and
R.D.
my center and my belief.

CONTENTS

INTRODUCTION

Not so long ago I was ambling along Manhattan's 56th Street. I had finished a few chores, unglamorous ones such as picking up photographs for my newspaper column, and I still had a few hours to kill before a dental appointment. Not exactly a stellar day, so I was dressed in a blue button-down collar shirt, jeans and sneakers. Suddenly a public relations woman for a much-heralded menswear designer wrapped her arm through mine (she seemed to have materialized out of the air): Was I free for the next couple hours? Sensing a free lunch, I allowed as how I was. Flash, we were taxiing to the designer's triplex on Beekman Place for an "informal" press preview of his latest collection. Not surprisingly, other men's fashion reporters and editors were at the luncheon, although presumably they had not been plucked off the street. Also not surprisingly, I was the only person in jeans and sneakers. After the showing, as I was excusing myself to go to "my next appointment" (considering the surroundings and the occasion, admitting that I was going to have my teeth cleaned seemed too mundane a confession), an associate editor at one magazine couldn't restrain himself, while pointing at my jeans and sneakers, from gasping, "Dressed like *that*?" Mustering reserves of wounded dignity, I smiled, squared my shoulders, exited and walked directly to see my dentist, who wasn't the least affronted when I appeared minus designer-signature-buttoned blazer and imported Italian shoes.

Unfortunately, the widespread notion that so-called *fashion* equals snobbism can often be validated. But even the most egalitarian among us don't expect theatergoers to arrive in bathing trunks. Standards of appropriate attire for particular occasions have become entrenched and are commonly accepted. Should we make an error in judgment, we should remember that down-the-nose, haughty stares are downright rude. When *fashion* becomes elitist, it's a bore designed for boors. Some room for individuality must remain, although (I admit) jeans and sneakers are wrong at a fashion show. As a guideline, if you don't want to dress to the expectations of the crowd, don't go. (I shouldn't have, but I'm a sucker for free lunches.) But don't feel overly constricted either. Today, rules are far less ironclad than during Victorian times. It's always better to be yourself than a caricature of a stuffed shirt.

So why be concerned with fashion at all? Isn't a preoccupation with appearances inherently superficial? Isn't who a person is, not what he wears, what really matters?

The truth is, whether we like it or not, appearances do count. And how we're dressed, rightly or wrongly, is one of the criteria used by others, right or wrong, to peg us. Redefining some of our attitudes about fashion might change our minds about making clothes work for us.

Most men's ideas about dressing right are created—possibly warped—by men's fashion publications. Such media thrive on presenting what's "in" or "trendy." Season after season they offer a smorgasbord of looks that may conceivably look appetizing on their pages but that appear too concocted when worn on the street. Many fellows, reticent about *fashion* to begin with, don't have the stomachs to try the fare. They become increasingly queasy about the idea of dressing right by associating it with *fashion,* so the gap between what they're seeing in the fashion publications and what they're wearing gets wider and wider. Only the brave ones go the distance. *Fashion* becomes polarized.

At the same time, the men's fashion magazines try to show the new styles in relatable, if fanciful, contexts. Clothing is tagged for business or for weekends or for formal events. Business generally translates into business suit. But what about the man whose business centers on arriving at the factory to take his place along the assembly line? He would be mocked if he showed up daily in a banker's pin stripe. Weekend often translates into either slacks and a Harris tweed jacket or silk loungewear. But who dresses like that washing the car or cleaning the attic? Formalwear translates into an ambassador wearing tails to a diplomatic reception. But what about the groom-to-be whose fiancée pines for an unusual wedding motif? He'll rent, not buy, his tuxedo, which more than likely will be in a style and color ridiculed by traditionalists.

The fashion publications and many of the designers, cognizant that they are not reaching mid-America (how bitterly the phrase falls from their tongues), retort that *fashion* was never meant for the masses and that men of taste are always ahead of the times. Meanwhile, the majority of bewildered men simply give up. They abdicate any responsibility for their appearance to the women in their lives. They feign indifference. They have more important things to worry about, or so they assert.

Truthfully, of course, these guys do care. But they perceive (in many cases correctly) that they have been abandoned by *fashion*.

When mystiques are wiped away, men's fashion really refers to men's clothing. Nothing more, nothing less. Anything that any man wears, whoever he is or how much the outfit costs, represents *his* fashion. Whenever he dresses, he is making his personal fashion statement. And he should realize the simple truth of the matter.

The first step in dressing right is to recognize that clothing (as opposed to abstract *fashion*) is an extension of yourself, not a conspiracy with loss of self as the ultimate goal. Dressing right is not the be-all and end-all, but it's potentially as much *you* as your personality (which can shift according to what you're wearing), your job (which determines what you wear a great deal of the time), and your body (which can be visually altered by what you put on).

How can someone use clothing to his best advantage? Well, *fashion* has so complicated the scene that an answer doesn't come readily. One fellow might choose a particular suit because he thinks it will help him gain entrance into the board room. Without the raw intellect, guts and ability required, no way. Another guy might want clothing to turn him into a great lover. If he avoids deodorant, fat chance. Still another man might expect clothes to restore his lost youth. Even plastic surgery can't do that. Putting clothing into correct perspective is necessary. A new wardrobe will not work miracles. But it could give a visual and emotional boost, which ain't bad. Using clothes to look better is in and of itself enough. You needn't rationalize further.

Rather than following trends or fads, before buying even one more tie, the man who wants to dress right should learn the time-honored principles of balance and proportion to use as guides for putting the pieces of his wardrobe together for best advantage. Often the change of a collar style or a tie's knot can make a tremendous difference in the total packaging of oneself. Dressing right is no more than having the pieces fit correctly. And since men are different, dressing right will be different for different men.

But given the years that men have spent avoiding looking after their own appearances, isn't learning now too difficult a task? Not at all. Neither biologically nor physiologically superior are women's eyes to men's; nor do women possess an innate sense of what goes with what that men by their birthright lack. They've just had more practice. The only effort involved for the male gender to comprehend how to dress right is the decision to open both his eyes and his mind.

Throughout this book you'll read about various clothing styles and how certain combinations work together while others don't. You'll encounter specialized considerations for tall men, short men, hefty fellows and slim ones, even for males with bowed legs or long necks. There will be hints about mixing pattern with pattern, color with color, and for achieving liberal, conservative or bombastic results. Obviously not every sentence will be explicitly applicable to you. Skip those parts if you feel like it. Better yet, read the information anyway. If you've been pretending that you don't care about how you present yourself, you have some mental catching-up to do. Seeing how the principles of balance and proportion work, even under conditions not your own, will help in your overall understanding of dressing right.

There are several ways you might read this book. The first option—and one not recommended—is the lazy cop-out. Simply flip to page 16, scan the paragraphs about different body types, then analyze yourself to determine which one you are—Stocky Endomorph, Athletic Mesomorph, Stringy Ectomorph, Y-Shaped, Pear-Shaped or Rotund. If you don't correspond closely to one of these types, mentally cut yourself in two at your waistline. Are you more akin to one body type waist-up and closer to another waist-down? "Mismatched" bodies occur all the time. Or, are you fairly "average" with only a slight inclination toward one body type? Not everyone is easily and irreversibly assignable to a mold. In either instance—if you combine two body type tendencies or if you have only an unpronounced inclination toward a type—you will have to temper the clothing advice accordingly.

Having analyzed your body shape, now you could simply jump to the "Index" to locate the listing for your body type. You could write down all the pages entered under it, then methodically check out only those passages. Of course, following this routine would be boring, and you'd miss more than a few bits and pieces along the way. You'd also be bypassing many principles for piecing together a handsome and workable wardrobe.

Actually, this slothful way of using the book is one of the final steps in the recommended way to read it.

A more useful approach is to take *Dressing Right,* both the book and the subject, at a more leisurely pace. Read it relatively slowly and absorb the thoughts as you go along. Yes, after digesting the material on body types, do a strip-and-mirror number. Decide what body type you are closest to; if you combine two tendencies or are an understated example of one, mentally take note and file the information in the back of your mind. For a while at least, remove yourself from the scene. Read on, immersing yourself in the theories about dressing. When you come across a reference applicable to any body type, slow down to analyze how balance and proportion are achieved. Keep your visual imagination attuned. Understanding how clothing affects all bodies will arm you better to target your own needs.

From time to time, you may encounter a term (perhaps the name of a particular fabric or pattern) you're unfamiliar with. If not knowing it doesn't interfere with the sense, forget about it. For the time being. Or, if you want to satisfy your curiosity immediately, insert a book marker (I shove in a matchbook) and turn to the index, which is clearly cross-referenced. You'll probably be referred to a page in "Spare Parts"; this section contains discussions and definitions about various clothing styles, patterns, fabrics and assorted nitty-gritty.

After proceeding from "Premise" (with its rundown on body types and generalized strategies for dressing according to body proportions) through "The Principles" (guidelines on texture, color and pattern) and "The Looks" (a rundown of several clothing options) to "The Wardrobe" (hints about planning for optimum flexibility) to "Practice" (assertive ideas about shopping), you'll encounter "Body Works." Here you'll find a breakdown of specific body types and precise suggestions of which styles are best for each body type in everything from suits to swimwear. Particulars about clothing styles are further detailed in "Spare Parts." ("Spare Parts" is designed not only as a reference point, but also as a section to ramble through during spare moments to learn some hard-core information as well as some trivia to unleash at cocktail parties.)

Over three hundred photos are interspersed throughout these pages. They weren't plopped in for the hell of it. Each photograph illustrates at least one aspect of dressing right. Whereas women are persistently sizing up other women, many fellows avert their eyes when another male enters the room. Dumb. One way to educate our eyes is to use them. Enjoy the excellence of the photographs but dissect the principles shown in the outfits as well. Notice the play of textures, the relationships of patterns and tones, the expected and unexpected combinations. Investigate seemingly small details such as collar pins and pocket squares, the way a scarf is tied.

Dressing right comes only after the decision that you want to. It's as much a mental process as assembling the right wardrobe pieces. If you resolve to get it all together (your outlook included), then you won't be a victim of *fashion*. You can be a strong-willed participant on your own terms and turf. So what if fashions change? You'll be prepared to change *what* you want *if* you want. So, study the photos, not to copy them but to decide what you like, what you don't, what viewpoints are applicable to you and how to work out your own interpretations. Don't automatically discount what's unfamiliar until you familiarize yourself with what's going on.

Now, with all this material under your belt, should you decide you want to use clothes to make the most of what nature passed your way, you can do what the lazy person did first—use the index to track down references to your specific type (or types) and to review the advice, accepting it, rejecting it or adapting it.

Reviewing yourself, too, never hurts en route to dressing right. Every six months is a new fashion season. The times change as you do. One reason many men find dressing right a hapless chore (and one too often left unattended) is that we're mainly dressed by others. As infants, our mothers chose our booties, and they may still be choosing our shoes and socks until we pass ourselves into the hands of girl friends, wives or lovers. As kids we had our "for-good duds," which we wore religiously for special occasions and religiously got out of as quickly as humanly possible. We felt silly, discovered by our grubby cohorts when we were in our Sunday best. We developed a resistance to clothes in general and to the "right" clothes in particular.

Well, the "right" clothes are those that make us feel good, not uncomfortable with ourselves. But so many of us just aren't giving clothes a chance. Believe it or not—and you should—dressing right in the right way with the right attitude can be a natural high. Really. But you've got to be personally involved. Looking good isn't self-importance; it's self-respect. It's also fun. Nothing more, but that's a lot. The days of passive resistance should be over. If you want to look better—and who doesn't?—it's time to stop avoiding the issue. You're the moving force. Move.

PREMISE

THE FIRST STEP
ANALYZING YOURSELF

HELPING NATURE

BODY LANGUAGE

No one likes to look bad.

But a lot of men are skittish about admitting, even to themselves, that they want to look better. Why? Because we've been taught that any concern about the male appearance is misdirected vanity.

Junk that thinking. It's old hat and off base. Healthy vanity is just that, healthy. We're born with it and we're frustrated if we don't express it. True, looking good and dressing right don't rate high on the scale of World Significance when compared to eliminating famine or avoiding nuclear holocaust. But daily pursuits and worries are seldom of world-shaking consequence. So let's not take our wardrobes—or ourselves—overly serious. On the other hand, let's not treat our clothing—or our outer selves—as unworthy of notice either. Perspective is a saving grace.

Confessing that he hadn't read a newspaper in months, one lionized menswear designer quipped, "I should reform. I'd hate to miss out on a new design trend because I hadn't known about a war." Narrow thinking.

Urging men to be more aware of how they dress, another menswear commentator resorted to fear tactics when he remarked, "You may never have a second chance to make a first impression." Logical, but again the perspective is askew. Too inflexible.

One clearly-honed statement about how clothes work best comes from Coty Award-recipient Sal Cesarani, who notes, "If we couldn't speak a word, our clothes would do the talking for us." The correct perspective: clothes communicate. They tell others about us, how we view ourselves and how we hope others will view us. The associations are automatic and ingrained. The phrase "banker's suit" conjures a particular image, usually of someone dressed in a navy suit, a white shirt and a conservatively striped tie. Obviously not all bankers wear that outfit, but the outfit suggests authority and reserve. We make assumptions about the person wearing it. Time and closer contact may prove us wrong, but the clothing has sent out signals.

John Weitz has commented, "Clothes do not make the man. Brains make the man. Charm

makes the man. Achievement makes the man. But clothes can be a positive comment, a pleasing statement, a tasteful expression."

He's partially right, partially wrong. If we relied exclusively on clothes to express who we are, we might as well be paper dolls. But we're not all men of brains, charm and achievement. We're human beings, too often muddling through, doing the best we can. We want acceptance from others. Like it or not, how we look and dress are the only clues strangers have to assess us when seeing us for the first time. Then. As time goes by, people hopefully know us, not only our facades. But, ironically, how we dress can change both our facades and our inner feelings. Another Coty-winning menswear designer, Alexander Julian, points to the paradox: "You may need confidence to wear a certain outfit; but by wearing it, you gain confidence."

Fine. But where does one find that sense of self-assurance, particularly when clothing oneself?

We've got to create it if it doesn't exist yet. And only we can do it.

Gone are the days of the 1930s and 40s when *Esquire* could decree the fashion do's and don'ts for every event and every season. Sociological changes in recent decades have smashed any supposed fashion dictatorship. Nor do we any longer receive our image of men's fashion from Hollywood. Cary Grant and Fred Astaire were role models back then, but no one has succeeded them. Designers have their own conceptions, often at odds with each other. From time to time we hear a heralding of a surging trend, such as a return to elegance or to the finely-fashioned man, but few people, if any, buy that. Eclecticism in male wearables is here to stay.

So should you skip it and just continue wearing what you have been wearing? Sure, if you want to. "If you don't view what you wear as something fun and interesting and just something to fool around with, then fashion is not your thing," suggests Don Sayres, one of the women's wear designers who entered the menswear scene in the late 70s.

But if you keep what you wear in mind and what it can—and can't—do for you, then clothes are worth more than a passing thought. Yes, some effort is involved. But few worthwhile things come free.

The starting point is having a perspective on yourself. A lot of people talk and write about self-image. That's only part of it. And a lot of self-deception can be involved. Before getting off on your mental and emotional You, there's that physical being that genetics and happenstance gave you and that other people see. First, train your eye to look at yourself as if you were a stranger. No, that's not right. Because you should be standing nude (or in briefs) before a full-length mirror, and that usually isn't how strangers experience their first encounter. But forget that you've ever looked in a mirror before, because you probably haven't done it in the way you should be looking at yourself right now.

Make an honest assessment. Are your shoulders broad, narrow or average? What about your chest? Is it muscular or tending toward softness? Your waist. Does it swell out to your chest measurement? (Don't worry about finding a tape measure; just compare the visual proportions.) Are you hippy or flat-assed?

After assessing the obvious, scrutinize the less apparent. What about your neck? Is it stubby? Is it long? Are your legs or arms shorter or longer than normal?

Check out any and all idiosyncrasies. And don't panic. How the phrase "the average man" was ever coined is a mystery, since more atypical physiques exist than typical. Nonetheless, a basis exists for classifying body types. One approach is awesomely called *somatotyping,* which refers to the morphological (another winning word) aspects of the physique.

BODY TYPES

Fundamentally, the hypothesis is that all human frames can be categorized according to their similarities to the three basic somatotypes.

THE ENDOMORPH

The endomorphic frame has a relatively prominent abdomen and generally tends toward a certain softness or roundness of the body parts. Musuclar development does not appear prominent, although the person may be very strong. Rather, endomorphy is simply the body's natural and genetic tendency toward "softness" in outline. An extreme or exaggerated endomorph would have a sizable round body (sometimes euphemistically described as "stocky"), with a rather squat neck and shortish limbs that are fleshy at the

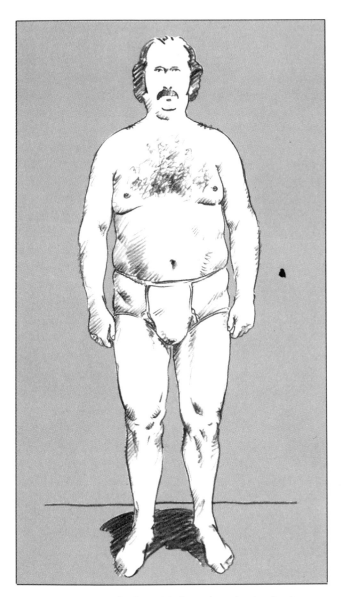

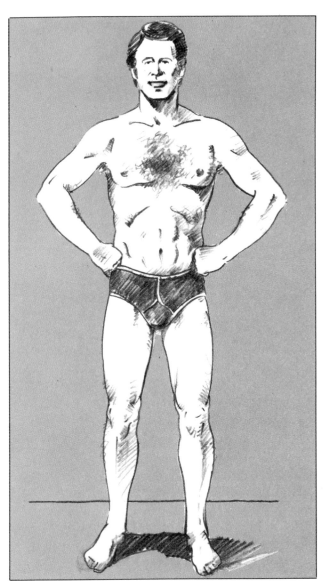

upper arms and the thighs. A relatively larger amount of overall body fat may be present, but this alone does not determine endomorphy. In fact, an underweight person could still be considered an endomorph.

THE MESOMORPH

In contrast, the mesomorphic frame is bonier but more angular, more muscled. It is what is typically called an "athletic" build, since the musculature—or the appearance of musculature—is the body's most visibly pronounced feature. Characteristically, a decided mesomorph would have brawny shoulders and chest, with highly developed arm and leg muscles and minimal body fat. Of course, the mesomorph can be overweight; mesomorphy, like the other somatotypes, is a

natural tendency which may not be fulfilled to its inclination. However, while muscle can be built on any body through exercise and a strenuous physical regimen, if an individual is not a born mesomorph, he cannot achieve true mesomorphy.

THE ECTOMORPH

The ectomorphic frame might best be called "stringy." An ectomorph is typically lean and may look hungry. Muscular development appears lineal as opposed to full-bodied. In fact, a high degree of ectomorphy exhibits narrowness—a tall and thin body, long and thin limbs, next-to-no body fat. Going against his natural tendency, an overweight ectomorph would appear puffy or blown-up, since the excess flesh would make the frame virtually disappear. Following the natural

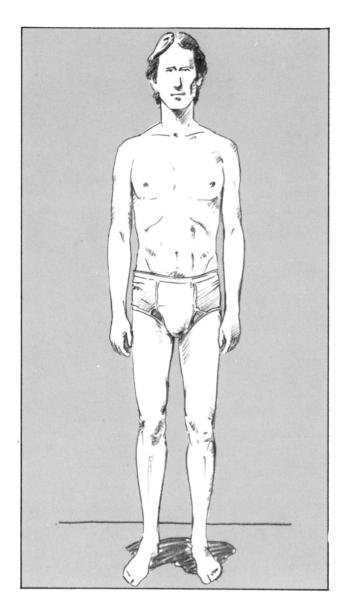

between clothing and the wearer's body. The most glaring example is what occurs when a stocky endomorph flouts his girth and emerges wearing an oversized plaid. On the other hand, the contours of his ample body are de-emphasized, everyone knows, if he wears a chalk-striped suit. Not so immediately apparent is that the suit will appear still more slimming if it's made of a fine worsted wool rather than a heftier, thicker fabric.

tendency to the extreme, ectomorphy would approach emaciation.

Of course, in life, assigning people to one of the three somatotypes isn't all so tidy, since we're the offspring of random mating and not cloning. Nor does the somatotype theory presuppose that men can be definitively pegged by type. Instead, the hypothesis is that men and women come in all shapes and sizes with many variables, but that all human forms can nonetheless be analyzed in relative terms against the three prototypes.

Also pivotal to the theory is that, after puberty and rarely before, one's somatotype is unchanged by diet, exercise or age. Speaking plainly, we're stuck with what our biological parents passed our way.

Since clothing, when worn, is on a human frame and not a hanger, a specific relationship exists

The latter adds bulk at the same time the vertical lines of the pattern are valiantly trying to create the optical illusion that this stocky guy is in better shape than he really is.

Or take the string-bean ectomorph. Obviously vertical stripes will only make him appear taller and thinner. But so will tight jeans topped by a dark and drooping cardigan sweater worn over a muted plaid shirt, all of which conspire to turn his frame into an inverted exclamation mark. To fill out his frame—visually if not actually—this fellow might wear the same basic items (trousers, sweater and shirt), but put a light-colored turtleneck under a beefier plaid shirt and tuck both inside pleated, full-cut pants.

These two illustrations share an underlying assumption, that the most desirable physical appearance is that of the athletic mesomorph, or at least some approximation to those proportions. The prefix *meso-* is derived from the Greek *mesos,*

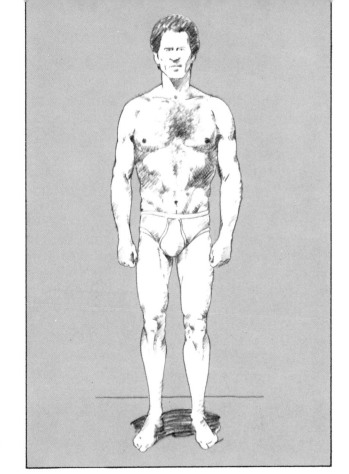

meaning middle; *meso*morphy is the middle ground between endomorphy and ectomorphy. And so the athletic mesomorphic stature is considered the Ideal Norm for the male body.

Few men naturally fit into the mold of the Ideal Norm, just as very few are pure examples of stocky endomorphy or stringy ectomorphy. Still, and over the years, the Ideal Norm remains the physique of classic proportion and balance, of symmetry that's eye-pleasing. Can clothing help a man suggest that he is built along the Ideal Norm's scale? Well, clothes can try.

But since physiques vary so greatly, the classification of body types only by the basic stocky, athletic and stringy frames is insufficient for drawing generalized conclusions about clothing one's body to best advantage when compared to the Ideal Norm. After all, "mismatched" bodies are the most common types around.

So-called mismatching occurs between the body's torso (waist up) and the lower portion (waist down) of the body. Suppose the top of the body is very pronounced, with broad shoulders and/or an accentuated chest, but the waist and hips are very slight. This effect might be aesthetically pleasing to some; however, when the top-heaviness is too emphatic, someone can look apish. Either way, to approximate the Ideal Norm, the visual trick is to minimize the top, maximize the bottom. (How to will be discussed at various stops throughout the book.) Making up a new somatotype, this would be

an endo/ectomorph—or someone with a *"Y-Shaped"* frame.

Conversely, bottom-heaviness—an ecto/endomorphic or *"Pear-Shaped"* frame—is almost never

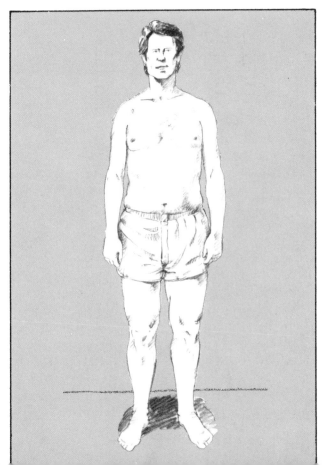

aesthetically pleasing. When the unbalanced area is a man's midsection, a guy may appear beer-bellied. When the bulk is misappropriated to the hips and thighs, the visual imagery is that the fellow should waddle. The sought-after result for both is the same—to refocus the eye to the top at the purposeful expense of the bottom. Although anomalies won't disappear, they can be belittled.

The final newly-coined somatotype would be a man with a nonexistent physique. Call him *"Rotund."* Unlike the stocky endomorph, who has a natural tendency toward roundness, the rotund man has given into that tendency with a vengeance, no matter what his somatotype originally might have been. He doesn't bulge in the wrong places; he bulges everywhere. His physique is the most difficult to reproportion visually.

From the three basic somatotypes—Stocky, Athletic and Stringy—three more have been

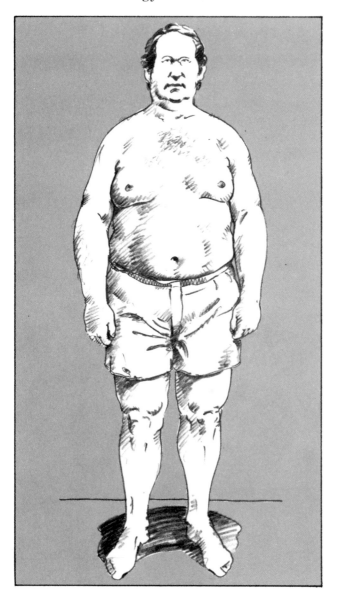

derived—Y-Shaped, Pear-Shaped and Rotund. Since the Athletic physique (or bodies roughly corresponding to it) already comes relatively close to the Ideal Norm, a man possessing it can wear nearly any style of sane clothing he likes, and maybe even some that cross the borderline.

BODY STRATEGY

STOCKY ENDOMORPH

Overall, the emphasis should be on the vertical line. Similarly, the relationship of top to bottom should be as continuous as possible, meaning strong contrast between attire above and below the waist should be avoided. This is especially true at the waistline. The worst possible error (and one of the most commonly committed) would be wearing a white belt with a brightly-colored shirt and contrasting trousers. Individual apparel items will be examined in later chapters, but for the stocky man, the over-riding guideline is: keep the clothing in the background, your head and face in the foreground.

STRINGY ENDOMORPH

Clothing emphasis need not necessarily be horizontal, but it should not be vertical unless a man perversely wants to accentuate his linearity. Contrast above and below the waist may be very desirable, so long as it doesn't simply split the man in two. Very dark/very light is less workable than a muted palette of softer contrast. The stringy man can be more adventurous in layering an outfit, which always adds weight. *Layering* is a dressing technique of adding two or more layers of clothing to the torso. For example, a man might simultaneously wear a sweater under a shirt, topping both with a vest, even another outershirt or a jacket, and perhaps tossing on a voluminous muffler for good measure.

Y-SHAPED ENDO/ECTOMORPH

Contrast works well here because the body itself is already in a contrasting state. When the body's imbalance is downplayed, so is its idiosyncrasy. Strong pattern or color should be reserved for the lower portion of the anatomy, in an attempt to make the top less dominant. Fine, never bold,

stripes on top will sometimes work toward this end. Finer, lighter textures should be relegated to the top; bulkier fabrics to the bottom. The goal: weight inversion.

PEAR-SHAPED ECTO/ENDOMORPH

Just the reverse of the foregoing. When the upper torso is outweighed by the waist and/or hips, the body needs some visual straightening out. In this instance, filling out the top and drawing attention away from the bottom will help in the rebalancing. However, layering on top, though adding bulk, could be dangerous if not carefully executed; the man might end up looking just plain bulky overall. It's wiser to rely on lighter colors or plaids on top, dark solids on the bottom, to create the wanted illusion.

ROTUND BUILD

The man who finds himself with this configuration should direct all his efforts into shaping up and only then address his thoughts to making his clothes work. First there is the body, then come clothes. However, if for some unaccountable reason a fellow can't shed enough pounds to allow a bone structure to emerge, a few—very few—ploys exist for camouflaging his shape or lack thereof. However hard he tries, though, he can't even come close to approaching the Ideal Norm. The ploys? The same as his stockily-built counterpart, the

endomorph, but carried out in more detail: no hat brims wider than moderate; shirts whose collars have slenderizing long points; no wide ties; shoes with no toe decoration. Less is more on this body type.

However, let's pull back from these ideal types. There is a relativity within each category. A mesomorph can still have a paunch. A mesomorph he remains, but with endomorphic tendencies. All advice, then, must be tempered with this slight duality: mesomorphy has the upper hand, but endomorphy is trying to reach in.

In life, we are seldom all one way or another. That's individuality. And bodies are as individualistic as personalities. Recognize that the Ideal Norm offers guidelines, but guidelines that only you can interpret. Earlier you were told to study your body. Well, do so again, with even greater deliberation.

HEIGHT

While men's body tendencies can be categorized according to these six types (admittedly loosely), other physical characteristics must be considered. Height is the most apparent one.

A man with a short but stocky physique, for example, may find a working solution for his clothes that a tall, stocky fellow wouldn't choose. Consider trousers. The shorter man might select a

pair of fine-wale corduroy slacks in a medium-dark shade because of the heightening quality of the fabric. But the taller, stocky individual might find no clear advantage in wearing that vertical line in the trousers (although it would still be fine) and would instead select a pair of classic flannel pants. Similarly, the two might lean toward different sweater styles to wear with their different bottoms. The shorter man might opt for a medium-dark, deep V-neck sweater with some striped detailing outlining the V, so the eye is drawn upward toward his face, which will now be geometrically framed. The taller man might want a crewneck sweater only slightly lighter or darker in shade than his trousers. It might also have some decorative detailing, but this time around the crewneck, so the lineal line would be a bit broken while the waistline would be underplayed in favor of the neck area.

Or: two stringy bodies, one short, one tall. The shorter fellow wants to look taller, whereas the taller one doesn't necessarily care. In this case, the smaller man might emphasize vertical lines but would simultaneously try to broaden his physique. Incompatible goals? Not if he wears nubby herringbone trousers, which add some bulk even with their verticality. The tall stringy fellow, though, might be better off in plaid pants with some horizontal interest, perhaps a houndstooth-type check. On top, the shorter male could consider a shorter-than-normal cable-knit cardigan, which

would continue the vertical line but would still be somewhat hefty in its proportions. But his taller counterpart might well choose a turtleneck, ski-influenced sweater with a horizontal treatment around the chest, filling out his dimensions there.

Examples could come unendingly. The significant point, in theory preceding practice, is that clothing not only creates a visual relationship with the body, but that individual pieces worn together likewise affect each other. Proportions shift and change as the components shift and change.

But back to the Ideal Norm. Basically, the concept presupposes that it doesn't really matter how you achieve it—you can assemble and re-assemble the clothing parts—as long as the Ideal Norm is kept in sight. As Chip Tolbert, the fashion director of the Men's Fashion Association of America, puts it, "A man can read the magazines, check out the stores, be up on fashion and buy the very latest thing, but if there's no balance, if the proportions are wrong, then he's still going to look like a schlump."

FASHION VS. STYLE

In truth, some menswear designers are at odds with the Ideal Norm theory.

Ronald Kolodzie, known for his innovative sportswear, remarks, "The more that I think rules exist for dressing right the more I find that the next day, or within the next few minutes, the rules can be broken." He goes on to say, "Really, looking good in clothes depends upon what you do with the clothes, not just the clothes themselves. Most people dress for others, but in a negative way. They say categorically, 'This won't work on me, that would be horrible on me.' They miss out on a lot of possibilities. So people don't dress in an exciting manner, because of fear of rejection. In actuality, the opposite turns out to be true. If a person takes liberties in how he dresses, without going outrageously crazy, then others look to him as being adventurous. They come to expect it, and would be disappointed if he didn't continue. So, instead of being rejected, he has more liberties, and no one stops to analyze, 'My god, his neck is too short.'"

Don Sayres echoes Kolodzie's sentiments, but expresses himself differently. "I think that one of American men's biggest problems in dressing is that we are too concerned about who we are, or think we are. People who are imaginative and who experiment with their dress are less restricted about life in general because they have fewer set ideas about how they want to present themselves to the world.

"You have to know who you are within your own mind," Sayres continues, "and who you are is different from what you look like. Identity is a mental process. It is dangerous when someone relies on his physical person to tell him who he is. Then you have a very rigid person, entrenched in looking only one way. I don't think that there has ever been a fashion that in some form or another couldn't work for everybody. Dressing is simply a matter of proportion. A man of any height, for example, can wear any type of clothing *if* the proportions are scaled down or scaled up to that height. It just takes looking in the mirror and deciding where that look, on you, should start and end. Any rule that says that you can't do this or you can't do that is ridiculous. If someone does it well and creatively, he can wear just about anything."

But that's the whole point: *if it's done well.* Excess creativity can become oddball. The Ideal Norm is based as much on mental rules of proportion as physical ones. Likewise, a balance must be reached between a man's frame and the framework of how he wants to see himself. Then, when he absorbs that self-image completely, it becomes part of his personality and is reflected in how he clothes himself.

Polo's Ralph Lauren states, "Confidence that you're dressing right will make a mistake look right." That philosophy also relates to the Ideal Norm—unless there's self-delusion. The Ideal Norm is self-knowledge. Which brings up the question of the difference between being fashionable and being stylish. Or being neither.

Being fashionable means wearing clothes at the time they are in fashion. Period. You may not look good in them, but you're "in fashion." Having style is looking good in your clothes whether they are in or out of fashion. "The stylish man is very fortunate, because if he wears what happens to be current, he'll look like a million dollars; and even if he doesn't, he'll look like half a million dollars," reflects Bill Kaiserman, creator of the costly, high-fashion Rafael line of menswear.

In general, according to the principles of dressing right as outlined here, clothes should labor less to create a fashionable look or a personal style than a balanced impression. The right clothes may be stretched to incorporate fashion influences, but, foremost, they are adapted to a body, not a trend. And, of course, to a personality, not a herd instinct. Bodies vary. Personalities vary. Clothes that are right for one man's body and personality are wrong for another's.

DRESSING RIGHT

Being well-dressed is a subject unto itself. Is it being fashionable? Trendy? Understated? Inconspicuous? Attention-getting? Is it finding a good look and sticking to it? Is it a matter of personal, even eccentric, style that has nothing at all to do with the actual clothes a man is wearing?

Since fashion is a chameleonlike creature, fashion's creators have their differently-shaded points of view.

Bill Blass
"Being well-dressed has to do with appropriateness, and that's why the cowboy is the best-dressed man in our country."

Pierre Cardin
"The well-dressed man makes the most of his body contouring. He clothes himself with a sense of style and flare, but in a way that accentuates his body and makes it appear more athletic. Today's fashion is coming out of comfort. Still, there must be shape. Shaped clothing is always more flatter-

ing to the physique, as opposed to mere body covering that someone puts on only because it's big enough to button."

Sal Cesarani

"Whatever anyone wears automatically has a sense of style; the clothes say, 'This is who I am, this is what I represent.' When men buy my clothes, they are not buying my image of them; they are buying an appearance for themselves in their own image. An image is very necessary for every individual, and basically that's what being well-dressed is about. The other term for image is style. The hungry fashion savage—and there are few of him—is the guy who needs to go out and wear something new. The average guy dresses to continue an image. Whatever a man wears is his own fashion statement."

Alan Flusser

"In English tailoring, to be able to spot someone's suit down the street is an anathema. Really standing out in the crowd vulgarizes the concept of dressing well."

Luciano Franzoni

"What's most important is not to look phony. When every aspect is too carefully put together, a man looks unreal. Dressing well should be fun, not hard labor. I dislike anything that smacks of putting a man in a slot, a uniform. Dressing well is being an individual."

Alexander Julian

"People with a great deal of personal style can appear well-dressed by virtue of the ease with which they display their clothing. Generally, a well-dressed man never looks out of place, as opposed to most people who consider themselves well-dressed when they are really over-dressed. A three-piece suit at a picnic looks out of place as does a bathing suit with a black tie at the opening of the opera."

Bill Kaiserman

"Certain people have presence. I've seen people who at the base are not overly well-built but who look absolutely fabulous in fashion, and I've seen some perfectly-proportioned models not look so great in fashion. Presence makes the difference. Personal style has to do with feeling absolutely one-hundred-percent comfortable. If someone is so comfortable in what he's wearing, you look, because it's one, the person and the clothing, never two. You don't judge the person naked and then the person with clothes. The clothing is the person. If someone is not comfortable with the way he's dressed at any particular moment, then he's not well-dressed. If he doesn't believe in how he looks, that doubt comes through to others and he looks dishonest, a fool."

Ronald Kolodzie

"All men live fashion, whether they realize it or not. Forget those people who say, 'Oh, you look awful.' If the people you want to attract think you're sexy and are turned on, then you just keep going on the route you've chosen."

Ralph Lauren

"The well-dressed man knows who he is and dresses to express what he stands for. When he gets up in the morning, a guy thinks he's an Ivy Leaguer, a Western Cowboy, a Rock Star, whatever, and then he fills himself into that image at that particular time."

Bert Pulitzer

"A truckdriver dressed like a redneck, with the right black and white wool shirt and the right hat and the right chinos, looks as well done as a guy wearing a three-piece suit on Wall Street. If you take hunting-world, or survival gear, and when you see a man wearing it on Fifth Avenue, he looks *chic*. To make that look *well-dressed*, he would have to be out in the country hunting."

Don Sayres

"As with anything else, in dressing well the most important awareness is timing. You get the term 'trendy' as something bad from people jumping into things just too soon without letting a look evolve or grow for them. But if they wait too long, then they're out of fashion. No changes in clothes or fashion should completely overthrow you as a person and the way you have been dressing. On the other hand, I detest dressing in a way that hangs out a shingle and says, 'I am an art director or a doctor or whatever.' No one has to dress according to others' expectations."

Robert Stock

"Looking good is an attitude. It's how you carry it off. Being well-dressed? Realizing where the game is at and then if you want to play it but not necessarily buy it. Then you know you're doing it as a fun trip, you're not taking it too seriously, and then you come off very, very strong. Attitude."

Egon Von Furstenberg

"There is a way of dressing for each age. If you stick to it, you always look the best. If you try to play another role, you look the worst. If a man is fifty and puts on a flower-printed shirt with a pair of jeans with studs, he's going to look the worst. The better way is to wear things as simple as possible, just wearing good quality clothes."

John Weitz

"Fashion is of a time, and so is being well-dressed. In 1942, a military uniform looked more fashionable than a business suit. What soldiers do with their uniforms proves who has style and who hasn't. Generally, men shouldn't be overly courageous, though. What's worse than seeing a red jacket walk into a room, shouting, 'Hello, I'm a red jacket; guess who I'm wearing?'"

CLOTHING CONSCIOUSNESS

Despite the differences in vocabulary and attitude, when one reads between their lines, each designer is really saying that for a man to be well-dressed, he must discover how clothes can work best for him. But learning how is a bit chicken-and-egg: what comes first, the clothes or the man? Can—indeed, should—clothing patterns which reflect personality patterns be changed, since personality and clothing apparently are so intertwined?

Clothing patterns should be changed if someone wants to change how he appears to others. That sounds simplistic, but it's true nonetheless. Almost every male could dress better than he does. Presumably most would want to dress better if they only knew how. Or would they?

The psychology of clothing is more complex than one might suspect. First of all, why do we bother to dress? Laws are one reason. But most statutes merely stipulate coverage, not the type of coverage. For protection against the elements? Possibly, but that explanation also fails to answer why we choose particular modes of protection—jeans and sweatshirts or suits and ties as opposed to sacks—to protect our bodies.

Centrally, we clothe ourselves because we're expected to, and we tend to wear what has come to be expected of us, in order to win approval. Clothes are one currency we use to barter with others for

their affection, because if we stubbornly refuse to dress in a manner acceptable to them, then odds are that those others will overlook us, or look upon us with some mixture of mirth, alarm, ridicule or contempt.

One of the difficulties in choosing how to dress is deciding whom one wants to please or court. Is it a lover or a corporation, one's peer group or the group one aspires to, or simply for one's own pleasure?

A quasi-truth seems to be that most men want to dress pretty much like the other men with whom they have contact. Certainly any member within the Chic Pack dresses either like the rest of the pack or in an outrageous manner that other pack members will still consider chic; to look ordinary is criminal here, yet there is an ordinariness in their extraordinariness. A stroll into gay haunts will find the gays hunting in similar attire; to stand out is to look as if you're in the wrong bar, and that you should get yourself into the right one. Saturday-night bowlers are easy to recognize with their matching team shirts and one can also see graphically who the enemy is. Cover the faces in most corporate dining rooms and you'll be hard-pressed to name any names.

Yet, while many men want to be associated with their group and employ clothing as one instrument to do so, a little vanity usually creeps in, some flicker of independence. These fellows, while wanting to look like their peers, also want to stand out from them ever-so-slightly.

How is this clothing dilemma resolved?

By facing it straight on. By thinking just as much about *why* you dress in a particular way as *how* to dress with more personality. If the two motivations won't come together, choose one or the other as valid for you; you can't pursue both ends.

DRESSING SMART

Using clothes to rebalance the body to correspond as closely as possible to the Ideal Norm does not presuppose that only one look prevails for any one individual man. It does hypothesize that certain shapes, patterns, colors or styles of clothes can look better together than others and that some clothes look better on certain men than on other men. But options are always open. One option is to ignore the guidelines. In fact, one current highly-touted fashion gambit suggests always wearing one item of apparel slightly at odds or off-beat with the overall outfit. Then, the notion goes, you will have more credibility than if you were too packaged. Maybe so. You could also look extremely affected. Proper execution matters more than the purity of a premise.

Face it. Being fashionable has its risks as well as its rewards. What one person considers fantastic some other will think looks disastrous. And what appears bravely avant-garde to some can inevitably seem boringly passé to someone else. There's no way that you can win with fashion if that's what you want—universal approval. And with no infallible arbiter on what looks right and what looks wrong on anybody, you might just as well assign the judgeship to yourself. If the search for the Ideal Norm should ever become confused with the quest for the Holy Grail, rethink.

Yes, clothing does communicate. Yes, clothing does comment on you. Yes, clothing makes you more acceptable to some and less so to others. There are status associations, group associations, sometimes wrong and unfair associations. But the idea that you cease to exist outside of clothes is dumb. Sure, clothes should have "credibility," "personality," and then some. So should you. Clothes should appear spontaneous. They should never be a drudge, or a drudgery. You are more important than your clothes, always.

The Ideal Norm statement is as much an anti-fashion as a fashion statement, because fashion and dressing right are often incompatible. Looking stylish can also battle dressing right.

Fickle fashion cares not a fig about the state your body is in. To achieve fashionability, the only mental exercise required is in discerning trends—accurately.

Alternately, dressing with style is predicated on the force of your personality. The only emotional exercise is to develop presence—naturally.

But to dress right, your body is the focus—initially.

When narrow lapels are in fashion, to dress fashionably, you wear narrow lapels as long as they are in, but no longer.

To be a stylish dresser, you wear wide or narrow lapels as you choose, when you choose, believing your self-assurance will carry you through, even if fashion, your body and your decision are all at odds.

To dress right—that is, by following the principles of the Ideal Norm—you wear wide or narrow lapels, depending upon which style complements your body better, so your body and your lapels can sing in two-part harmony.

Of course, if wide lapels are the better personal choice in terms of the body language of the Ideal Norm, but if narrow lapels happen to be in fashion today, wearing wide lapels won't win you a place on the best-dressed list. Today. But you won't appear on a worst-dressed compilation either. Ever.

Either way, or either list, what does it matter? A little or a lot, depending upon what you want from clothes.

However, don't make the mistake of believing that clothes can sell you. They can't. And you wouldn't want them to. If you ever put yourself on auction, you will doubt your own worth. Beneath those clothes, your body is still there, and it remains as real as you are. Looking good or dressing right isn't betraying yourself; it's exhibiting pride and displaying self-respect.

For the moment, though, suspend judgment about whether you want to dress fashionably, dress stylishly, or dress right. Each alternative will necessitate your becoming more intimately acquainted with your wardrobe anyway. Just keep in mind that clothes are a means, not an end.

Find all the joy available. And give it back.

PART 1

THE PRINCIPLES
ACQUAINTING YOURSELF

Too many crimes of neglect are committed by the uncaring.

Not that dressing wrong qualifies as a felony, but doing justice to one's appearance is a simple act that makes the world, and oneself, more enjoyable. Unfortunately, indifference often remains the unmotivating force behind many a man's self-presentation.

For someone with only a dab of knowledge, the male wardrobe can be bewildering territory, since it ranges over so much ground.

Yet today few men can afford to own several different wardrobes for all the facets of their lives. They require that dress clothing can occasionally be recast to do some downkey performing and that sport clothes can from time to time take on more upbeat roles. Individual items of apparel, supposedly in different moods, must be gregarious companions with other clothing items for any wardrobe to operate efficiently. But talking of wardrobe planning puts practice before principles.

We've been told that nature abhors a vacuum. Similarly, articles of clothing don't exist, for practical purposes, in isolation. In a chest of drawers, a dress shirt has no real meaning. Worn on a man's body with a tie, with a suit, with shoes and socks and other miscellany, then that shirt becomes part of an outfit that represents the wearer at that particular time. At another given moment, the shirt or any of the outfit's components can be separated and reassigned to new outfits, where it takes on a new significance.

How a piece of clothing adapts to new couplings depends upon both the character of the garment itself and the nature of the assembled outfit. To stay with the dress shirt example, the shirt alone might look like a champ; but with the wrong tie, the wrong suit, the wrong shoes and socks and miscellany, the pedigree shirt looks like a mongrel. Obviously, purchasing this spectacular shirt or that fantastic pair of trousers isn't enough. An understanding of how the pieces can form meaningful relationships must come first.

Any garment, be it a bow tie or a bikini, shares three common elements with every other piece of clothing. Each has *texture* (the physical and visual "feel" of the garment), *color* (even if the color is neutral or a so-called noncolor) and *pattern* (in the loose sense that a totally one-hued garment is still "patterned" by virtue of the weave or knit of the fabric).

Bow ties and bikinis come in a variety of styles. Reaching for mutual compatibility between them might seem ridiculous on first thought, since the two don't belong together. Normally. Shirts and pants do. Presumably. But if the texture, color and pattern of a shirt fight with the texture, color and pattern of a pair of pants, so much for their togetherness. For the time being, forget about what items are natural or unnatural duos.

Grab several articles of clothing (which ones won't matter) and drop them in a pile. Ignore whether a garment is a jacket or a jock strap. Place a couple of these pieces side by side randomly. Then make some switches. Concentrate on how the textures, colors and patterns look differently in different combinations. Keep playing. And studying. If you feel like an imbecile, don't. Do the exercise anyway. Watch what happens. Be receptive. Seeing a yellow sweat sock (or a yellow whatever, since it doesn't matter what the article is) next to a blue and red dotted silk tie (or whatever) might remind you how crisp and cheerful primary colors can be together. The pairing of a muted check shirt and tweed deerstalker's cap could surprise you with the warm tactile sensation, pleasant to the touch as well as the eye. Perhaps you'll notice that two different stripes on who-knows-what don't do battle but look like life-long buddies.

Maybe you're the one man in thousands who threw a bikini and a bow tie into the heap. Let's suppose you are. You'll never wear them together, and no one's telling you to. Still, the bow tie is woven of homespun wool in chocolate brown and olive green plaid, with a gray silk neckband lining and the bikini is a khaki and tan stripe. Maybe in a flash you've seen how three textures, five colors and three patterns (counting the silk weave as a pattern, in addition to the stripe and plaid) can all work together in close harmony. Maybe you've envisioned an outfit made up of a brown and green, roughly textured wool shirt worn with khaki pants sporting a gray ribbon belt around the waist. Where did the khaki pants come from? From the khaki colored stripe in the bikini. Free associate it into a pair of socks.

Of course this exercise may be, and probably is, asking too much. Perhaps— probably—that mound of clothes wasn't so inspiring. Yet. The trick is using your imagination. It's waiting to be tapped. Use your eyes. They're lazy, conditioned to taking it easy. The more you look, the more you'll see. The more you look and see, the less elusive dressing right becomes.

For now, don't get bogged down in minutia, such as wondering if you have enough suits. Who cares? A hundred suits are a hundred too many if they go badly with everything else in your wardrobe. More than anything else, making a go of one or a hundred garments depends upon the interdependence among texture, color and pattern. If these three aren't synchronized, be prepared for a rough flight.

Texture is a touching relationship.

Color works either by harmonizing

Patterns require attention to scale,

and brights energize.

Neutrals calm

or by contrasting.

an eye to color compatibility,

and occasionally guts.

Chapter

FEELING GOOD

*Texture is waiting to be seen
as soon as we focus our attention.*

SURFACE THOUGHTS

Often the simplest things come hard.

Texture is a surface thing. Literally. So there shouldn't be much to penetrate. Satin is smooth. Burlap is rough. These two fabrics feel different to the body and appear different to the eye. Every fabric has texture. So far, so easy. The going gets harder when combining textures.

The tactile nature of menswear has often been overshadowed by the more showy elements of color and pattern. A man may decide he needs a blue shirt or a plaid vest but will seldom stipulate that the shirt should be oxford cloth, a relatively coarser fabric than more finely woven broadcloth, or that the vest would be great if made of a woolen fabric, with a gutsier, fuzzier finish than a smooth-surfaced worsted one. It's not that he takes texture for granted; he forgets about it.

Texture is so self-evident we may not see it. Although we seldom sharpen our vision, when we bother to look closely we notice immediately that denim jeans have a definite diagonal furrow in their weave that creates a texture different from poplin pants with their fine horizontal ribs. Texture is waiting to be seen as soon as we focus our attention.

Understanding texture is not an abstract exercise without practical application.

Dressing right is a celebration of the senses of sight and touch. In many ways, our eyes touch as well as see. When something is "velvety soft" or "smooth as a baby's bottom," we don't need to feel it with our hands, our eyes can do the discerning for us. The touching relationship involved in what we wear—the interplay of textures—contributes as much to dressing right as compatible colors and pleasing patterns.

Similarly, texture does as much to affect body proportions as color and pattern do. Take a burgundy and navy small checked kimono-style robe. The unobtrusive colors and patterns can be worn by nearly any man without negative consequences. Let's say the robe is made of silk. Very debonair for lounging about. But too smooth for the stringy ectomorph if the surface texture is flatly understated. The same robe in a shantung silk, with a nubbier texture, would work harder to counteract his linearity. More texture gives his body more apparent substance, even when the colors and patterns are exactly the same. Conversely, the smoother silk is more substantially diminishing for a stocky endomorph than the shantung.

When the kimono robe is worn with pajama bottoms, then the textures of both pieces take on new dimensions relative to each other and, of course, to the body the two are draping. Say the pajama pants are in the same shade of navy with a widely-spaced but fine stripe in the burgundy shade found in the robe. No color or pattern problems between top and bottom. But that surface thing, texture, also needs to be taken into account. In principle, the smooth silk kimono robe should look terrific with the pajama bottoms in velvet. On someone pear-shaped? No. The visual weight of the two textures—the lightness of the silk above the heaviness of the velvet—is in the same misbalance as the pear-shaped frame. Turn the textures topsy-turvy without altering another touch and the pear-shaped guy assumes better apparent proportions. On the other hand, a Y-shaped fellow would be better off turvy-topsy.

Depending on the surface arrangement of the fibers or yarns in various fabrics, different textures emerge. Now is not the time to distinguish the textural facades of fabrics and weaves. That information, as well as a complete menswear vocabulary, appears in detail in the "Spare Parts" section at the conclusion of this book; later check the Index under "texture," "fabrics," and "weaves" to locate specific discussions in "Spare Parts." First, tackle the broader issues. Dressing right is not unlike a jigsaw puzzle. Each little piece is part of the picture. Some pieces are more important than others and become building blocks. Once the building blocks are discovered, other pieces start falling into place. Finally, when all the pieces are put together, the total picture presents itself.

BREAKING DOWN

Until the latter 70s, textural interest in men's clothing hadn't amounted to much for decades. An occasional burly tweed might have roughed up the suiting scene, but, for the most part, events sailed along quite smoothly. The pieces of a suit almost always came in identical fabrics. Then conventional suits started splitting apart. Designers presented some so-called suits that didn't look like suits at all. The jacket came in a different fabric than the vest which wasn't the same fabric as the pants either. Texture became more pronounced and prominent. "Pure" suits remained in the majority but were under seige from mixed breeds.

Reputable designers and manufacturers insisted that these pretenders were legitimate.

Even now, the notion that a suit's jacket, pants and vest may be unmatching is seen by some fashion conservatives as radical. Previously, elitists were sustained by the belief that where the aristocracy would go in suits, the bourgeoisie would appear in sport jackets. (A questionable generalization, but truth never concerns bigots.) If nonmatching suits, which look suspiciously like sport-jacket ensembles, should be accepted, what happens to symbols of superiority? Poor fashion fascists.

As menswear continues its break with tradition and evolves toward greater democratization, many time-honored tenets for dressing well no longer apply. Most old-guard rules were based on the premise that the rich and the privileged were role models for the lowly to aspire to. Too often this precept turned dressing oneself into a masquerade, with "unworthies" disguising themselves as "worthies." Clothes served to reinforce class consciousness, subconsciously if not overtly.

Case in point. For years the prevailing notion about texture in menswear was summed up in "smooth with smooth, texture with texture." The origins? Aristocratic. In the city, the "gentleman" wore finely tailored worsted suits (smooth) and silk club ties (smooth). Strolling about the manor, he wore tweed suits (texture) and homespun ties (texture). His servants wore uniforms of his choosing.

Today, smart fellows don't accept the rich-are-better premise. But, unknowingly, they still dress according to its outmoded implications.

Take the smooth/smooth, texture/texture dictate. Aesthetically, there's nothing wrong with it. But other, more liberated options are available. Instead of confining clothing to an either/or microcosm, view the world of menswear as vast. Texture's territory expands when examined by the degrees of contrast that, assembled outfits can rightfully exhibit.

MINIMAL CONTRAST

This is the most conservative approach to texture, epitomized by the smooth/smooth syndrome. Understatement—clothing communicating in muted voices—receives the nod.

Strictly speaking, texture/texture can also fall within the confines of this approach, since contrast among the outfit's pieces is still negligible if all are in the same textural dimension.

THE SMOOTHS

As the name implies, there is nothing coarse about this group of textures or the outfits put together from garments with these textures. Clothing fabrics are plain woven without ever having tricky surface effects. The man who dresses with minimal contrast in all smooth textures supposedly projects authority and reserve. He is "safe" in dress and in image. However, this pervasive theory of image projection shouldn't necessarily be accepted at face value. Half-truths have a way of perpetuating themselves until they reach mythic status and become accepted as inviolate.

Do certain outfits project authority because men of authority wear them, or does the wearing of a certain outfit make a man authoritative? Logically, a person with a powerful personality expresses himself powerfully, whatever he wears, simply because he asserts himself.

To wield power over others, however, raises another question. Others must first entrust power to the wielder. Does how a man dresses predispose others to endow him with power because he looks/dresses as if he will use the power responsibly? Certainly this belief is widespread. Power-seekers are told to dress in a way to win more power. Many try. Some succeed. By virtue of the clothes or their personalities or their abilities?

The principles of the Ideal Norm and dressing right aren't concerned with power plays. But certainly the whole mystique of image-dressing (dressing to promote an *image* within the corporation or social milieu in order to convey one's status) is self-perpetuating. That's one reason so many men are badly dressed. They are promised that if they dress in a certain way, then they will reap certain rewards. Maybe. Maybe not. These clothing commandments are never based on helping you look good. Dressing right is based on making you look better. It promises nothing else. Only you can decide which will make you happier, dressing in a manner to play the part or dressing in a way to look your best.

Anyway, back to texture. To repeat, the man who dresses with minimal contrast in all smooth textures supposedly projects authority and reserve. The more conservative the cut of his clothing and its coloration, the more authority and

reserve projected...as long as he keeps his mouth shut. Should he utter a few words, he might let slip who he really is and what he really thinks.

Imagery aside, minimal contrast in smooth textures can look good or bad, depending upon who's wearing it. It is a very wise route for rotund males whose bodies need no additional complications. Mismatched bodies will be badly served by this approach. Textural contrast is one of the surer ways of rebalancing. Color and pattern can only do so much. Their effectiveness is minimized without calling on texture to do its essential part.

THE SUBTLES

Adding more texture, but not going rough and tumble, is minimal contrast in the subtle vein. Linen is an outstanding example of a fabric that has notable surface interest without flaunting it. But since fabric types themselves vary in texture, which ones they nominally are matters less than what faces they actually present to the eye. Some linens might be identified as strongly instead of subtly textured. Subtlety is in the eye of the beholder. Nonetheless, subtle textures usually are a little hunkier than smooth ones, but are seldom as beefy as strong ones. Their weaves are looser, more open than smooth textures, but stop short of being very loose and open, a space occupied by strong textures.

Ensembles that contrast minimally with all subtle textures manage to project *some* authority and *some* reserve, but less of both qualities than if all the textures were smooth. Subtle textures are less hard-edged than smooth ones, hence are less austere. Relative to image-dressing, softer clothing presumably represents moral softness or a soft will. Reduced austerity in other contexts might suggest compassion and empathy, both of which are qualities outside the realm of image-dressing.

Wearing all subtle textures is no more helpful to mismatched bodies than wearing all smooth ones. Being in a contrasting state naturally, mismatched bodies require clothing contrast to rearrange themselves. Of the somatotypes, stocky endomorphs are the best suited to subtle textures with minimal contrast if the cut of their clothing is appropriate—larger proportionately on top, less full on the bottom.

THE STRONGS

Minimally contrasting but strongly textured outfits are the least acceptable in image-dressing. Since they evoke a feeling of the country, the

implication is that someone who tries to pass off this individualistic style as businesswear probably hasn't given his all to the company.

Overlooking the question of loyalties, image-dressing and the concept of dressing right agree that an outfit composed solely of strongly textured items is the most individualistic approach and the most difficult one to carry off. Strong texture always insists upon being seen. Lots of strong texture can vie for attention. From a strictly aesthetic point of view, when an entire outfit of strong textures is pulled off correctly, the look cannot be improved.

Interestingly, the image-dressing objection to allover strong textural contrast in dress clothes does not extend to casual clothing. Any textural mix is acceptable out of the office. Image-dressing isn't really concerned with what looks wrong or right in the insignificant frivolities of private life. In terms of dressing right, the principles of texture are the same for custom-made suits or jogging outfits. Thus, if the stringy ectomorph clothes himself head-to-toe in strong textures at either the opera or the Grand Old Opry, he couldn't dress better to build up his body dimensions. But any other somatotype except the athletic mesomorph should proceed with great care. Mismatched types should remember that the concentration of strong texture on any protruding flaw will make it stand out more.

Assuming you've got the physique and the sense of adventure, how is this look of all strongly textured pieces properly executed? (The smooths and the subtles automatically mix if their colors and patterns work together.) It's not easy. When in the same color tonality, strong textures alongside strong textures have a good chance of being agreeable. Patterns, if any, should stay in the background, since emphatic textures appear as patterns themselves.

When all is said and done, experimentation counts. After an outfit is put together, if one piece dominates the rest, it is out of place. A way of testing this is to stand before a mirror and squint. By doing so, you soften your overall focus. Should one texture (or pattern or color, since this is the way of double-checking them too) jump out, it is probably subjugating the others unfairly and to a disadvantage. Of course, if you want one texture to shout out, that's your choice.

SELECTIVE CONTRAST

In pursuit of dressing right, minimal contrast in texture is often supplanted by selective contrast. To the smooths a subtle or a subtle and a strong texture will be added. All strongs will be tamed by a subtle or a subtle and a smooth texture. What garments will be given what textural treatment will depend upon personal preference and the person's physique.

In dress clothes, the traditional approach is to play texture down, even when employing selective contrast. Suit textures seldom become strong unless the suit is worn away from the business milieu. Evening suits are seldom heavily textured. Selective contrast, then, is relegated to smaller surfaces, such as ties and vests.

The man who updates traditional viewpoints without totally breaking away takes a few more liberties. He will mix more textures, concentrating on the subtles but unafraid of adding a strong now and then on a big scale. Whereas the true traditional dresser would wear a burly tweed jacket only on the weekend, the updated traditionalist might wear one to the office.

In casual clothing, selective contrast is far more prevalent than minimal contrast, mainly because the garments by their natures are more liberated and are offered in a wider range of fabrications.

Before moving on to the next chapter, go back and review the photographs in this one. Since there's no color to distract you, note how texture truly should not be underestimated. It makes a vital contribution to dressing right.

Chapter

2

COLORFUL IDEAS

*Color is not all that difficult if initially
you remove yourself from the picture.*

NATURAL CHOICES

Nature proves that all colors are beautiful—and go beautifully with each other. When the trees of autumn are ablaze, who would defoliate half the leaves because red doesn't "go" with orange? In a field of wild flowers, who would weed out even one bloom because blue and violet "clash"? Only on manmade things do we impose arbitrary color prejudices. Before being taught to color his thinking in terms of the adult world, a child with a box of crayons will challenge the rainbow to match his creativity. As we grow older, the colors fade to fit with our smaller, drabber universe.

The most basic color limitation in menswear stems from the supposition that only certain colors are masculine. A blue suit? Masculine. A pink suit? Feminine. Of course nothing is truly masculine or feminine other than sexual organs. But like most everything else, clothing is imbued with sexism. So-called "masculine colors" are dictated for suits, but colors brilliant enough to shame a peacock pass the masculine test on the golf course. The underlying premise is that in the world of business, men must defend themselves in manly armor against the threat of a feminine (or

effeminate) invasion. Off duty, they can relax their guard. On the other hand, women can wear whatever colors they please, wherever they please, because they have no status to protect. Sweet. Until society screws its collective head on right, double standards and wrong-headed thinking will persist. Meanwhile, the world of menswear isn't all that black. One way or another, color has been infiltrating male wardrobes and even some board rooms, much to the dismay of the proponents of image-dressing, those self-righteous defenders of yersterday's status quo.

PURE THOUGHTS

Without color, we'd live in a gray world. Clothing without color would also suffer a case of the blahs.

Egon Von Furstenberg, in his personalized English, relates, "I had a marvelous story happen to me once. I bought a yellow jogging suit, because when I went in front of all the girls in college, everyone else had a navy or a red one and I was the only one who had a yellow one. And as I'm not that bad looking, all the girls were looking at me and I

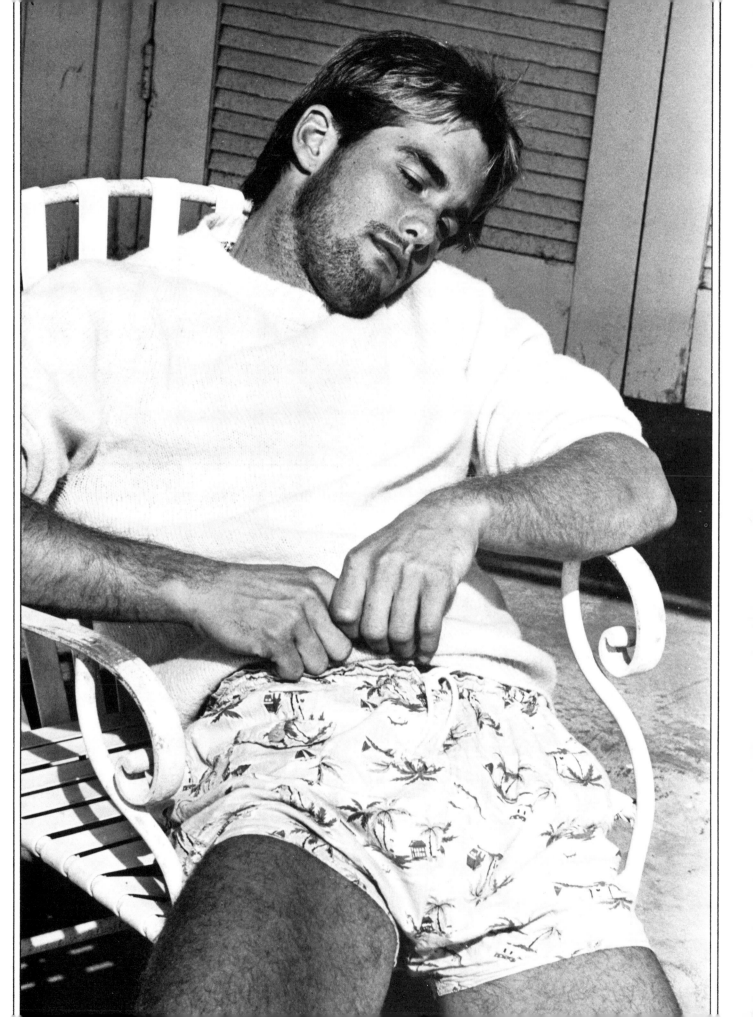

got all my dates that way."

Yes, color can make a man stand out in the crowd. It can also be a source of bewilderment. As Von Furstenberg goes on to say, "Mixing colors is where you see the most mistakes. I think if someone has no color sense, he should always stay in navy blue, gray and tan."

Another alternative is to develop a color sense.

Color is not all that difficult if initially you remove yourself from the picture. However, before looking at color in clothing, first you'll have to reacquaint yourself with some rather elementary information.

As you learned in grade school, all other colors can be produced by selectively mixing the three primary colors—red, yellow and blue. Equal mixtures of the primaries yield the three secondary colors—orange, violet and green. A mixture of a primary and a secondary color produces what is called an intermediate color, such as blue-green or yellow-green.

An invaluable device used by artists is the color wheel. Around its perimeter are the various hues resulting from an equal mixture of the adjoining hues. Scores of hues are represented. The basis of the wheel, though, is the eleven colors of the light spectrum. When natural light passes through a crystal prism, it is dispersed into these eleven "pure" hues—red, red-orange, orange, yellow-orange, yellow, yellow-green, green, blue-green, blue, blue-violet and violet. In nature, red-violet is missing from the light spectrum, but it is added as a basic hue on the color wheel, rounding out the number of pure colors to an even dozen.

Tertiary colors are mixtures of secondary colors. Tertiary colors can be mixed with each other, with primary or secondary colors, or with any other colors to create new hues. White and black can also get in the act. Color has infinite possibilities, but for now it's wiser to focus on the twelve pure hues to explore color relationships.

ANALOGOUS & COMPLEMENTARY COLORS

When the twelve pure hues are positioned circularly in spatial relationship to each other, the three primary colors are located equidistantly from one another, as are the three secondary colors. Falling between the primary and secondary colors are the six intermediate colors, likewise equidistant from each other.

Analogous colors are those that appear side by side. For example, five analogous colors centering around yellow are orange, yellow-orange, the central yellow, yellow-green and green. Furthermore, yellow-green, green, blue-green, blue and blue-violet are analogous colors too. They keep themselves in circulation. Analogous colors are always harmonious.

Complementary colors are direct opposites on the color wheel. Some opposing duos are yellow and violet, blue-violet and yellow-orange, red and green. These always contrast.

SOMETHING OF VALUE

We don't live in a pure world, so some new nuances must now enter the picture.

Add white to a pure color, it becomes lighter and brighter; add black, it becomes darker and duller. The relative brightness or lack thereof is called the color's *value. Intensity,* on the other hand, is an expression referring to a color's "purity." The value (that is, the degree of brightness or darkness) of two colors may be the same. However, if one color of the two has either more white or more black in it than the other, it is less "intense" than the color that fills the bill more naturally. In terms of color pigment, there is more of the "true" color in the intense color. The more true, the more intensity. In descriptive terms, a "vivid" color is more intense than a nominally "intense" one, which is more intense than a merely "strong" color; a "grayish" color is less intense than a "moderate" color. Brighter (also meaning lighter, relative to white) intense colors are more visually aggressive than darker (relative to black) ones.

Certain words cover both value and intensity: "brilliant" colors are light and vivid; "pale" colors are light and grayish; "deep" colors are dark and strong.

Colors also have moods. Yellows and oranges are cheery, evoking sunshine and warmth. Red is associated with fire, passion and excitement, sometimes violence. Blue is pacific, serene. Green is restful. Violet and purple are supposedly mysterious and sexy.

In most instances, reds and yellows are considered "warm" colors, meaning they tend to advance, while blues and greens are thought of as "cool" colors that recede. Warmer hues look even warmer when contrasted with cooler hues, and

vice versa. However, high-intensity colors, even cool ones, advance more than low-intensity, warm colors. For example, a brilliant kelly green comes forward with more force than a pale yellow, even though green is generally said to be cool and yellow warm.

So what does all this color theory have to do with dressing right? Think about it for a minute.

If your chest is barreling out, you certainly have no need of a sweater in a color that asserts itself into the foreground. Stay away from sweaters in brilliant warm colors. Pale cool colors are better. Dark cool ones are better yet. If your chest is concave, however, warm colors can't hurt.

INNER WORKINGS

Time for a little more theory.

Colors work together either by harmonizing or contrasting. That's it. Certain outfits can combine both principles in that some of the pieces will be in harmonious colors while others of the garments are in a contrasting color or two. It's the overall impression that counts. If the contrasting colors are found in a pocket square, the overall color scheme would still be harmonious. On the other hand, what difference does it make how any color system is named? No one is going to catch your act on the street and exclaim, "Wow, there goes a guy in a split-complementary color scheme!" Terminology is only a point of reference. Call a triadic complementary scheme Sally if you like.

HARMONIOUS COLOR

Harmony is the absence of any discord, when all parts interact in unity. In terms of clothing, several harmonious directions are open.

NEUTRALITY

Literally, neutral colors are achromatic, colorless. White, black and gray are true neutrals, although we commonly refer to them as colors. Neutrals can never be anything but harmonious; they haven't got it in them not to be.

Some colors we call neutrals aren't really. Pearl gray, for example, has a hint of pink, slate gray some purple. Often we think of browns as neutral. Yet browns also cover a wide range and can be green- or yellow-toned, to name only two of the numerous possibilities, which is why discussing color is so difficult. There is no way to judge abstractly how colors will look together until the actual pieces of clothing are put together. However, in the general terms of dressing right, the true neutrals—black, white, gray—and the quasi-neutrals—browns, tans, creams, oatmeals, beiges and colors in this family—are fairly safe bets for harmonious mixing.

Although neutrals should combine safely and can look marvelous (or sometimes monotonous), what are you really after?

Neutrals work very well with strong textural contrasts, since color doesn't complicate the issue. Similarly, several patterned neutrals may go well together, since the limited color range helps keep individual patterns in their place.

Neutral color schemes rate high on subtlety. They are very adaptable and seldom, if ever, look out of place, except in a gypsy caravan. They are equally at home in dress and casual attire.

Light neutrals—white, cream, pale gray, etcetera—on a large frame highlight the largeness; dark neutrals—black, deep browns and grays, etcetera—downplay size. When a body's proportions are split top and bottom, dark and light neutrals should be worn in the fitting split combination. For example, if you have a normally proportioned chest but pronounced hips with thick thighs, you will want to make the anomaly less apparent. A pale beige sweater with black pants should do just that. However, if the hips are very slender and the shoulders very wide (we should all be so unfortunate), then a deep gray sweater with cream trousers would work to eliminate some of the disparity. Naturally, warm and cool colors could also be called upon to solve the same problems. Warm colors act in much the same manner as light neutrals, cool colors like dark neutrals, in that light ones are more likely to advance, dark ones to recede.

MONOCHROMATICS

The prefix *mono-* from the Greek *monos,* meaning alone, should denote having only one color when affixed to chromatic. Sloppy as we are with language, the actual connotation isn't so specific. In clothing, monochromatic combina-

tions are almost never in only one hue used repetitively, or even in the same basic hue with some of the garments brightened with white or dulled with gray. Neutral outfits can be vaguely monochromatic, as can outfits in analogous colors, but generally monochromatic clothing revolves around various shades of a color. These shades contain touches of other hues but still belong in one family. The so-called masculine colors—the brown, blue, gray and green families—are nearly always the basis of a monochromatic approach in dress clothes. Pastels with lots of white are usually bypassed for more grayed, low-intensity hues. Supposedly feminine colors—red, violet, purple, to a lesser degree orange and yellow—are off limits, even in sportswear, for males dressing monochromatically, according to the traditionalists. Notice how cold colors in general are considered more masculine than warm ones. Could the implication be that "masculine" men are cold and emotionless? It sure looks that way. Hogwash. Color should be expressive, not repressive. If color can give anyone a lift, why not let it? As Sal Cesarani says, "Colorful clothes can make you feel good. When it's a terrible, rainy day, why not find the brightest yellow tie to make everyone you meet feel like saying 'Good Morning?' Color can cheer others around you. And yourself. Clothes can say, 'Hi, how are you? I'm in a spirited mood today.' Or they can say, 'I feel godawful.'"

What monochromatic clothing does for a man depends upon the amount of contrast and, of course, what pieces are in what color variation. Like neutrals, going this route is relatively safe, but it has the same pitfalls and rewards. The decisive factor is how contrasting the colors in the monochromatic scheme are. And, of course, the central color. Mismatched bodies are particularly affected by differences in color intensities. The pear-shaped fellow choosing a monochromatic green outfit, for instance, would choose a lighter, warmer shade of green with some yellow in it for the top and a darker, cooler shade of green with a hint of blue in it for the bottom.

ANALOGOUS COMBINATIONS

It comes as no shock that this way of using color in clothing is based on analogous colors, whose harmony stems from their proximity to each other. When only three analogous colors are used—out of the hat, pick blue, blue-green and green—the effect

is akin to a monochromatic scheme. If you use analogous tertiary colors, the effect is even closer. In color planning using limited analogous colors, it matters little how much of which color is used, the overall effect is still pleasing.

When you use five analogous colors, however, although the colors still act harmoniously together, the assembled outfit may lack focus if one of the colors doesn't predominate. Using a greater amount of the central color establishes a visual fulcrum. For instance, give blue the heavier load. Its analogous pure colors are violet, blue-violet, blue-green and green. Violet and green would be used only sparingly, perhaps as thin stripes on a shirt with a predominantly white (calming) background. Since blue-green and blue-violet are closer to central blue, these colors can be employed more assertively, perhaps in bolder stripes on a necktie or as checks on a pocket square, or both. Of course, the suit is blue.

Remember, to make the points more clearly, we are only using the pure colors of the light spectrum. When actually dressing yourself, it's dubious that you'll settle on pure red, yellow or blue, let alone red-violet, yellow-orange or blue-green, in full intensity as centers for many outfits other than casual ones, and then not often. But the principle of harmony remains the same—color proximity.

Getting back to what we've been told are masculine colors. Here are some of the hues that fit into analogous relationships.

BROWN: earth tones; khakis; oranges; bricks; rusts; maroons; etc.

BLUE: sky tones; burgundies; wines; clarets; various greens; celeries; etc.

GREEN: foliage tones; olives; mosses; various blues; ochres; golds; yellows; etc.

GRAY: any colors, since gray is neutral. Camel, blue, red and yellow are not uncommon mixers with gray.

White, naturally, is usually worked into any color combination.

CONTRASTING COLOR

Carried to an extreme, very strong contrast becomes discord, not very desirable in clothing combinations. Colors that fight with each other also fight for attention with the wearer. Since contrasting combinations are automatically strong, they are often toned down with neutrals or low-intensity shades of the contrasts.

PRIMARY CONTRAST

Since two or even three primary colors are called forth, this approach to color in clothing is the most vividly vibrant, traditionally applicable only to sportswear.

As noted, the three primary colors are equidistant from each other on a color wheel. If connecting lines were drawn between them on the circle, an equilateral triangle would be formed. This explains why the primary colors are described as a "triadic harmony group," though they contrast rather than harmonize.

The triadic relationship places equal emphasis on each of the three colors. But since all are equally strong to begin with, the proportions of their appearance are insignificant: a little or a lot of yellow, for example, in proportion to blue or red will not alter the basic bold impression.

Stringly ectomorphs or lucky mesomorphs are the only physical types who can confidently court such overall boldness. Since primary contrasts totally lack subtlety, they blare out any physical deviations from the Ideal Norm by giving the deviation louder, weightier expression. An athletically-built fellow can wear a brilliant red T-shirt and blaring yellow gym shorts and look great. A very tall and slender man will also shine. But put that show-off combination on someone rotund and he'll dazzle onlookers with his girth. His size is doubly emphasized by the two primaries. If the shorts were black, the effect would not be as bad, but the red T-shirt still points out his upper bulges more than a dark maroon would.

TRIADIC CONTRAST

Primary colors aren't the only trio to be found in contrasting relationships. Turn the equilateral triangle and discover new ones, such as yellow-green/blue-violet/red-orange. The secondary colors—green/violet/orange—are another perfect triad. Being mixtures of primary colors, these combinations are not fundamentally as loud-mouthed as the primaries, but in concert they're hardly ever soft-spoken. Tone them down with gray, thereby lowering their color value, and they become more muted. Yet they will still have the same importance and weight, so they can't detract from physical shortcomings either. To rebalance the physique, colors must be used in different balances. Triadic contrasts must be modified. However, triads are a way of identifying classical color combinations. Not that anyone can dictate that the classical combinations are the only ones worth considering.

SPLIT COMPLEMENTARIES

Another mouthful.

Since triadic contrasts are all in the same intensity, they risk becoming discordant. Although the three colors are supposedly clamoring for equal rights, in actuality each may be struggling for dominance. In clothing, if not in life, a *ménage à trois* of unequals can be more felicitous. Enter split complementaries.

Color choice is narrowed. On the color wheel, instead of rotating the equilateral triangle, an isosceles triangle gets turned. For instance, when the yellow/blue/red primary triad is modified into a split-complementary scheme, blue can get the top billing and yellow may be reduced to an intermediate status (yellow-orange), red, too (red-orange). Overall contrast becomes softer. In men's clothing, we're more likely to see this form of variation on the contrast theme because we're not accustomed to equal color rights in menswear. And, truthfully, split complementaries are easier on the eye than more strident combinations.

In general, color combinations, whether harmonious or contrasting, look better when a range of values and intensities are utilized. When planning an outfit, it is usually best to feature one color, at most two, using others in various measures as accents.

However, none of the guidelines or suggestions can ever replace experimentation. Yes, buying a color wheel at an artists supply store can help you literally see color relationships more clearly. But only if you play with it. Possessing it—or learning all the rules—won't guarantee success. Action is mandatory. If you're not self-involved—if you don't take risks on your own—where's the joy? Mimicry is a limited talent. Wouldn't you rather sing your own spontaneous song?

One sure way to get to the core of color relationships is studying winning combinations. The two color sections in this book offer several approaches, each one valid depending upon your needs, to combining color in menswear. Study the relationships picture by picture. In fact, closely examine the black and white photographs as well. They illustrate principles of shading and contrast. Naturally, all the photographs pictorialize the principles of texture and pattern too, while offering a range of styling alternatives. Although you might not like all—but hopefully at least some—of the outfits shown, the diverse guidelines for dressing right are at work in the illustrations. Learn from them...and from well-dressed men whom you meet on the pages of magazines or wherever your paths cross.

CHARTED COURSE

Since color occupies such a prominent position in clothing, almost no one is neutral on the subject. Many philosophies exist about personalizing one's wardrobe with color.

Concentrating the bulk of clothing choices in two related color families—perhaps browns and tans or blues and grays—and adding colorful bursts of energy in smaller doses is the conventional advice. It works, although choices can become somewhat predictable.

In larger wardrobes, a variation of the two-family tactic is possible. Create a basic wardrobe within the two related colors but inject a few major items in contrasting colors. Balance the contrasting elements primarily with neutrals, but add some brilliant small touches for extra dash. For example, the basic wardrobe pieces might be a brown flannel suit and a tan twill suit. A major item in a contrasting color would be a red tartan plaid sport jacket. Mixable, neutral elements would be gray and beige Shetland sweaters. But a lemon yellow sweater would add some brilliance while still fitting in with all the other components.

The central notion of this approach to color is that when all clothing has color compatibility in both harmony and contrast, then assembling the outfits attractively is ensured.

There is an entirely different way of looking at clothing and colors. One viewpoint is that for every individual, certain color shades are right, all others wrong. Judy Lewis, a former model, is one of the advancers of this notion. With partner JoAnne Nicholson, she devised a system—and a company—called Color 1.

As Ms. Lewis tells it, "Many color systems are on the market. None had the answers I wanted for myself. So, I started research on the subject, using a control study group to test what I found. My objective was to develop something factual and effective for each individual's visual enhancement. This went on for a seven-year period, and the research led naturally into my personalized color consulting business which has grown in the past five-and-a-half years to a national scale."

Her copyrighted color system for dressing is called "Personal Color Harmony." The basic principle is that every person can wear *all* the colors in the color spectrum in *some shade*. Ms. Lewis does not refer to colors by descriptive names (e.g., partridge versus slate brown). "This is greatly misleading to the public because usually they can't relate the name to the color. In my color charting system, everyone has his own shade of brown, simply called brown. So, instead of trying to name the brown, they just take their color sample in their shopping cart and match it up."

But first things first.

According to Ms. Lewis, "The skin color of people is their background color—their 'beige' color. Every color they wear should enhance and go with their skin tone. Every individual's body has a color scheme, which is the basis of his personal color chart."

While cautioning that "There is no such thing as 'average' coloring or a 'normal' complexion; *all*

coloring is unique," the color consultant does allow that people can be grouped generally into four color types, called "color harmonies."

CONTRAST COLOR HARMONY. A person with extremely dark hair and light ivory to dark olive skin (clear in tone, with a minimum of pink or yellow.)

MIXED COLOR HARMONY. Brown hair with bronze or reddish highlights, or red hair; the skin can be medium-light to medium or dark.

LIGHT-BRIGHT COLOR HARMONY. Golden blond hair, or light brown with golden streaks or highlights; or darker brown hair with golden streaks or highlights; golden skin tone.

GENTLE COLOR HARMONY. Ash blond hair, or medium to dark brown hair; light, pinkish skin.

"A so-called Scandinavian blond could be one of two types," remarks Color 1's cofounder, "a Light-Bright or a Gentle, depending upon the golden or pinkish tones in the skin. Each type would need to wear different shades of colors and different combinations."

She asserts that her system works for all people, saying, "Skin tone is the main determinant, regardless if a person within an ethnic group has predominantly dark hair color." Black skin tones, for example, may tend toward either the rosy or yellowish; very dark hair may have more red or more golden highlights, Ms. Lewis points out. Even if hair is dyed, a person's color type remains constant, since presumably a good coloring job will be compatible with an individual's natural skin tone.

A person's coloring and color type, claims Ms. Lewis, determine how bright, clear, muted or grayed their shades of colors need be. Coloring also dictates whether someone can wear extreme contrast combinations or should wear soft contrasts. In general, to dress according to her theory, *Contrast* types can wear clear colors and extreme contrast combinations: they should avoid wearing muted colors and analogous or monochromatic color combinations. *Mixed* types can wear muted or brown-toned or dusty colors; requiring soft contrast combinations, they should avoid extreme combinations and clear to bright colors as well. *Light-Bright* types can wear bright colors or combinations of medium-value extreme contrast; they should avoid muted colors and blended or one-color combinations. *Gentle* types need to wear soft-toned or grayed colors and can best wear soft

contrast combinations, as well as related or monochromatic looks; they should avoid bright and clear colors plus extreme light-dark contrast.

"Individuals often have personal color preferences that are wrong for them," states Ms. Lewis, "principally due to enculturation. We never really see ourselves objectively. Color preferences are 'head trips.' Some very few people intuitively like a color that is good for them visually without realizing why it is good. They choose it by accident or trial and error and use it without definite purpose."

Not everyone, she admits, is ecstatic with the results of the analysis. One client whose red color turned out to be a pinky, dusty, rosy shade moaned, "How the devil can I be a devil in that anemic red?"

OTHER SHADES

Most designers take a dim view of such a definitive approach to color in clothes. Here is a sampling of their thinking. Plus a final summary from the Men's Fashion Association's fashion director.

Bill Blass
"Stay away from yellow, especially if you have sallow skin. There was a period when American men were caught up in the most acid yellow shirts and green suits. But there wasn't a man in a thousand who could afford to wear those colors. Most men don't realize that an ivory or an off-white shirt is more flattering than a white shirt if your skin isn't the best. You can only afford a dead-white shirt when you've been in the sun for weeks. Since a man doesn't have the advantage of makeup, or any kind of cosmetic help, he's got to choose the color of shirt that really and truly is becoming either to the color of his skin, his eyes or his hair. The same is true of ties. Brilliant blue eyes? Go for a blue shirt every time."

Pierre Cardin
"Remember what color you wore when you got the most compliments, then wear more of it."

Alexander Julian
"People with stronger complexion and hair colors can wear stronger colors."

Bill Kaiserman
"Don't overdress. Use colors that blend, that almost mute together, not those that contrast. And not colors that match exactly. Naturals of various sorts—from rust right down to beige and off-white, khakis and tans and different shades of brick—generally look good on all men, regardless of their coloring. Black looks fine on all men. So does gray. But I don't particularly like light-skinned, light-haired men in gray. Gray can easily be substituted by brownish or tannish colors in the same neutral feeling."

Ronald Kolodzie
"Color isn't separate; it's part of the whole. People should think, I am what I am, and I'm fabulous, and then dress that way."

Ralph Lauren
"Breaking rules is what I believe in. But to break the rules you have to know what you're doing."

Don Sayres
"Men tend to lean toward certain colors. Too much so. Say someone likes brown. He overdoes it. He owns a brown flannel suit, a brown and beige tweed suit, et cetera, et cetera. Now, there is room in his wardrobe for a color unlike all the others. Maybe a navy blue blazer belongs there for a change. Or at least another color in a sweater, so he won't get boring. To say nothing of getting bored. Add a shock color to break the monotony."

Robert Stock
"I think that white is a beautiful color that men don't wear enough."

Chip Tolbert
"There used to be one fashionable color per season. Well, that is passé. There are so many different shades and subtleties in colors that nearly any man can wear blue, gray, brown or certain shades of lovat, because of the mixtures. That's the secret of finding the right color—finding the right color mixture. Which ain't easy."

No, it ain't easy. Which makes dressing right worth pursuing. If every decision were programmed for you, you could realistically pass yourself off as a computer. And feel nothing. Making your own personal stamp creates stronger feedback.

Chapter

3

PATTERN PLAY

*The classic guideline for mixing patterns is that
no two patterns should be in the same scale.*

TOGETHERNESS

A New York men's fashion photographer is fond of repeating his own aphorism: "Sometimes you can get so cool you freeze your ass off."

Apt when it comes to dressing right.

To date, pattern players have been in the adventurous minority. Pattern's most deft proponent in this century was the Duke of Windsor, who remains the epitome of male stylishness to many.

"Mixing patterns takes a certain style. Very few people have it. We know the Duke of Windsor had it," analyzes Bill Blass, "even though his taste might sometimes have been questionable for his particular stature. He violated almost every rule for small men. The oversized knots. He would wear a bold pattern with another pattern and with yet another pattern. He was often thought by his father and a great many people in England to be garishly dressed. But he got away with it because he had an enormous authority about himself."

Sal Cesarani elaborates on the point. "Mixing patterns depends upon the aggressiveness of the wearer. The Duke of Windsor was the most aggressive in his mixing because he had a tailor who would tell him, 'This is right,' and he

possessed a highly-developed instinct about what he wanted to create for himself as himself. He was not only aggressive in his fashion, but in his lifestyle—in his decision not to be a king."

Because using pattern is the most individualistic aspect of dressing right, guys without royal bank rolls and custom tailors often ignore the subject entirely or rely on others to give a stamp of approval to their pattern gambits. Don Sayres believes many men, fearful of making mistakes, prefer being dictated to:

"When a whole outfit is displayed in a store—a jacket, sweater, shirt and tie, plus a scarf thrown over the shoulder—the store doesn't just sell the shirt. Most men come in and want to buy the outfit exactly the way it is. If something is hanging from the pocket by mistake, they want that too. A lot of men don't know how to mix a striped shirt and a polka dot tie. The sad part is their wives don't know either."

Know-how doesn't miraculously materialize out of desire. It comes from concentrated application. And risk. "Security," chides Alexander Julian, "is a blue blazer and gray flannel trousers."

Nothing's gained trying to build false security about mixing pattern. It's hard. But worth it. Some

guidelines will place patterning within closer reach, but grasping it all takes time and familiarity. And sometimes luck. Chip Tolbert admits, "I personally find it difficult to take a bold or definite plaid suit—say a strong glen plaid—and put a striped, let alone another plaid, shirt with it. The look is great. I've changed my shirt five times in a morning trying to master it. And I'm supposed to know what I'm doing."

On the other hand, what's so horrible about making a mistake? You won't be pummeled.

It won't be easy, but let's try to get some perspective on patterns.

CLOSE INSPECTION

The classic guideline for mixing patterns is that no two patterns should be in the same scale. A small pattern, a medium-sized one, plus a pattern on the large scale are preferable together to two or three patterns of the same relative size. One variation of this guideline is: if patterns contain the same elements, they should be in the same scale as they appear in the other patterns. For

example, picture a rather complex plaid. The background of the fabric is a small brown and rust check. Superimposed over this check in a lattice-effect is a sizable windowpane plaid in a deeper brown. Along either side of the vertical lines of the lattice are fine stripes in brick. With this plaid, any of the elements—the check, the windowpane plaid and the stripes—could mix if their original scale were retained. Of course, if all of them were combined without any solid-tone alleviation, the results could be tough to take. Or the results could be terrific. All would depend on what patterns were worn on what garments in what textures and what colors. Given all these variables, no wonder many guys find pattern-on-pattern exasperating. Keep plugging.

UNEQUAL EMPHASIS

In suit or sport-jacket outfits, the usual tactic for mixing pattern scales is either a "moving in" or a "going out" relationship between the shirt and the jacket. Assume you are mixing three stripes. If the stripes on the jacket are widely spaced and on the strong side, then the striping of the shirt will generally be finer and closer together. The patterns are "moving in" in proximity from outer (jacket) to inner (shirt) layer. In reverse, if the wider, stronger stripes are on the shirt and the closer, finer stripes are on the jacket, then the patterns are "going out." In both instances, the tie would be diagonally striped with balanced, alternating broad and narrow stripes-on-stripes.

This unequal emphasis on scale is the classic approach. The geometric progression is very orderly, neat and compact. Contemporary usage of multiple patterns often seems more thrown together. Not, of course, that it truly is. It is designed to be more challenging to the eye by being unanticipated. When stripes, the easiest patterns to work with, are the basis of pattern-on-pattern in the very current mode, lots of them are often piled on in very similar scale. Plaids, too, the most difficult to combine, become purposefully brash in their scale proximity.

Whether this more playful, iconoclastic approach to pattern scales will survive more than a few seasons as a fashion influence is anyone's guess. Although this tactic does loosen up pattern strictures, iconoclasm can be carried too far, and its punch smarts like a slap in the face.

Still, the last word on scale is: you won't know until you try.

TEXTURAL MATTERS

Pattern-on-pattern is usually, though not always, accompanied by strong textural contrasts, especially when executed in the contemporary manner. Changing the surface interest from garment to garment not only underscores the basic ploy but also helps to dispel any impression that an outfit is prepackaged. Various patterns of the same fabrication smack of all the garments coming out of the same cellophane bag.

When considering what patterns to mix, don't forget that even one-hued garments have a degree of pattern from the weave or knit of their fabrics. Wide wale corduroy has a striped effect. So does herringbone, with some extra details on the side, so it's a pattern-on-pattern in its own right. Some tweeds can appear as mini-checks or as unstructured patterns. Texture adds new dimensions.

In sportswear, pattern and texture can acceptably run the gamut together. Since the most accepted business suit remains the navy worsted, sterotypic thinking continues to equate emphatic textural and patterned deviations as oddities in the business world.

COLOR COMPATIBILITY

Given the numerous shades of any given color, saying colors should be compatible is much like saying that we should all be friends. Indisputable. And impossible. Color principles must be reexamined in the light of pattern. Harmony is of the utmost importance, particularly in dress outfits. Spectrum hues are just too strong in most patterned combinations. Madras jackets and primary pants may be worn by the country club set or on the campus, but that's about as far as they conventionally go. Only on rarest occasion is madras asked to do a pattern-on-pattern number.

Pattern-on-pattern need not be a daily dress habit. If so, it becomes as predictably monotonous as appearing day in, year out, in solids. Likewise, color compatibility should not preclude a surprise color or two either. As long as the surprise isn't too much of a shock.

Often when combining patterns men make the mistake of believing that all colors in each separate pattern must exactly match the colors in the others. Not so. Again, this appearance is too prepackaged. Subtle blendings and variations in value and intensity are more appealing.

Let's take three patterns: a houndstooth plaid; a very small pin check; and a reasonably pronounced stripe. And select three colors: blue; green; and orange. In pure hues, the colors would be too much. So let's choose some subtle, muted shades. A dusty gray with only a hint of blue. A deep, nonintense forest green. And a toned-down rusty shade of orange. We'll put together a sport suit look using related separates.

The jacket: the nubby houndstooth check with a background of dark beige (not even one of the three central colors but one that blends with them all); the checks in rusty-orange and forest green.

The vest: the pin check predominantly in dusty gray and tan but with flecks of brick and a slightly more vibrant shade of forest.

The shirt: oxford cloth, with widely-spaced stripes of dark brown flanked by mid-intensity orange and green very fine stripes on an off-white background.

The tie: a deep, burnt rust knit.

The slacks: gray flannel.

The socks: dark gray, heathered cables.

The shoes: brown suede wingtips.

Optional: a silk pocket square in a small paisley pattern combining shades of browns, golds, navy blue and emerald green.

None of the colors match each other exactly, but they harmonize closely. Also note the textural blending as well—the nubbiness of the jacket; the rough quality of the tweed vest; the surface interest of the oxford cloth shirt; the high-low depth of the knit tie; the nap of the flannel pants; and the smoothness of the silk pocket square.

All the key elements—texture, color and pattern—fall into line for kinship.

CONVERSATION PIECE

A master at combining color, pattern and texture is menswear designer Alexander Julian, who is not uncommonly seen in traditional dress clothes minus a pair of socks and who has been known to wear two ties layered one over the other and tied with one precise knot.

"If I'm going to a particular event where I want to look a certain way, I may try on four different shirts, jackets and ties," he remarks. "If I'm working on something particularly *nouveau*, I'll pull out ten shirts and fifteen ties, narrow them down to five, and then try them on. Some people think this is terribly affected."

Affected or not, doing so has placed Julian on the International Best Dressed List. But don't think his approach requires men to appear narcissistically vain. "A well-dressed man looks like the whole outfit was conceived bleary-eyed at the closet that morning, halfway by accident." He goes on to comment, "We're living in an era of anti-fop menswear, when you don't want to look too turned-out."

Still, his casual elegance is far from effortless. What's important is that the effort not show. And Julian does allow that too much effort to appear effortless can sometimes lead you astray. He likens this mistake to trying to dress when you have a top-notch hangover.

"The worst mistake you can make is to try to create something when you just don't have it in your noggin, when you're just not clicking," the designer says. "Well, I was going to this event, and I started experimenting with dark-toned shirts

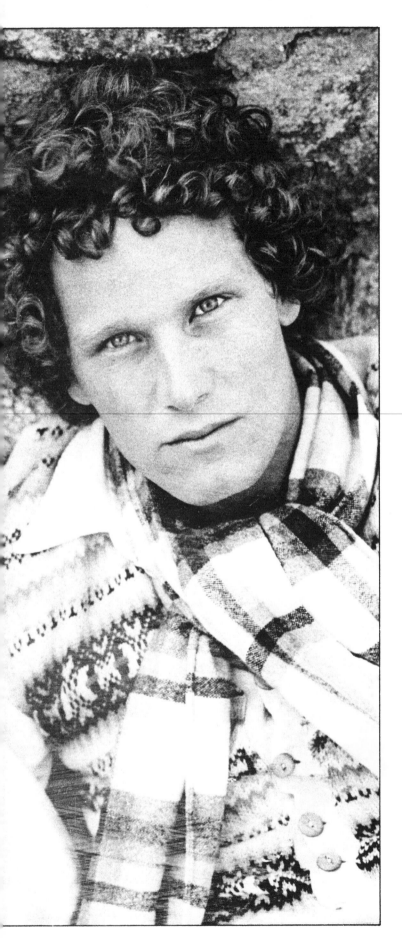

and trying to affect a certain attitude. I got dressed, looked in the mirror and thought, 'You are sick.' It's possible that the very same combination would have worked on another occasion, when I was up to wearing it, up to pulling it together and pulling it off.

"The more you have going on in an outfit, the more you have to be 'on.' Wearing certain outfits takes a lot of energy. If you're going to wear a bold overstriped jacket with a Shetland cowl neck sweater and a shirt and a scarf beneath it, with the jacket collar flipped up—if you're going to do a collar-up, pushed-up sleeves routine—you better have the wittiest answers to the first ten questions people ask you at the cocktail party. Otherwise, you're going to flop.

"If you're not up to the energy commitment, wear a dark suit."

Assuming your head is clear and that you have the energy to go the full distance, pattern-on-pattern, though evasive, is not impossible to capture. A conversation with Alexander Julian is a cram course on the subject.

What makes a man well-dressed?

"An understanding of the visible involvement that he has with the world around him. I think of people, men, women, whatever, almost as canvases. Things you wear can do the same thing as good paintings that challenge the eye and intrigue. But a well-dressed person never looks out of place."

Looking appropriate but still with some challenge to the eye?

"That's my particular way of doing things."

As long as the challenge doesn't go too far?

"Yes."

Is that what is commonly called someone's personal style?

"One way of expressing a personal style. I think being well-dressed involves a certain amount of personal confidence, a willingness to take risks."

How do men gain that confidence?

"Through knowledge of the subject. That's the only way to gain confidence. It's false confidence without knowledge. Aesthetic information has always been hard for American men to garner."

Are the principles of dressing well timeless or do they depend upon a fashion mode?

"There are timeless rules, but sometimes an aspect of fashion or style is to break rules. You have to be damn careful when you're doing it."

Are there timeless rules for mixing patterns?

"Let's say that there are timeless rules, but the acceptance of them varies according to the times. What we're doing with pattern in menswear today would have been unacceptable a decade ago."

Why?

"Because it was not being done. If it had been, it should have been done according to the same rules—the same attention to scales, et cetera—but since it wasn't done, people then would have thought that the outfits looked wrong. If it weren't for the explosion in women's wear with the peasant look—the whole eclectic approach, loads of pattern, color-on-color-on-color—we wouldn't have been prepared for pattern-on-pattern in menswear, at least not as far as it can go today."

Today pattern in menswear is less of a visual challenge?

"For people in the know."

And so it can become even more challenging to the eye and still be acceptable or appropriate?

"Exactly."

Where should men start when mixing patterns?

"The most obvious aspect is comparing the size of the pattern and, you might say, the pattern of the individual. A shorter person shouldn't wear wide patterns. A tall person shouldn't wear anything too stripey, too up and down. A tall, slender person can wear patterns attractively that no one else can. Plaid jackets with a horizontal influence, for instance. In most cases the vertical line is the most flattering for men, so most fellows have to avoid horizontals.

"A tall, slender person can also wear both bolder and brighter patterns and colors, although personally I like to classify bold as a four-letter word.

"There are only so few actual patterns involved in menswear—plaids, checks, stripes, twills, solids and tweeds. The tall, slender guy can take more advantage of them. And of sweaters with bolder horizontal striping. I don't think he should use anything terribly bold the higher up he goes on his physique. In neckties, which are vertically linear anyway, he should avoid brightness or boldness that emphasizes a strong vertical line."

But he can wear a bright plaid in a sport jacket?

"In jackets and sweaters both. The tall, slender person, like his counterpart, the short and slender person, is best suited to layers of things. That includes layers of patterns. Anyone quite thin should concentrate on using layers because he has the opportunity to do that better than most other people and can emphasize his individuality."

Does the short, slender person need different colors in patterns than a tall, slender man?

"No. But he'll need different patterns. Nothing with horizontal emphasis. Vertical plaids, interesting stripes, tattersalls or windowpanes that are vertically rectangular."

What about a tall, portly man?

"He's really got to pay attention. The parallel between the tall portly and the short portly is that old vertical line. Both should avoid heavy, heavy texture, and should go subtle in colorations and patterns, avoiding contrasts. Tight clothing is a disaster. It overemphasizes girth. But if possible, there should be some shape to the clothing outline. Shaped clothing needn't be tight. Although proper fit is awfully important, on a hefty guy pattern is even more crucial. If the pattern is wrong—too large or contrasting—this man can be fit to the nines and it won't do any good. If the pattern is right—small and non-contrasting—even if the outfit doesn't fit quite as well, the man will appear to be in better shape.

"I always think that a heavier person looks better with a vest because it moves your attention up to where the opening of the vest frames the face. Similarly, if a jacket is properly cut, it doesn't matter so much what's going on above the waist, since any movement there emphasizes the top of the male triangle. The most difficult thing to pull off is pattern-on-pattern when it comes to mixing patterns between jackets and trousers. I don't generally believe in patterned slacks unless they're tweeds. Shirts and ties are less of a problem. The size of patterns on shirts and ties doesn't do as much to change a man's visual stature as does the overall outside shape of the jacket or trousers.

"But back to vests. Vests on a big man—any man, really—should be in the same fabric or tone as the jacket or the pants. I don't like vests with lots of contrast. And certainly not with pattern-on-pattern, if someone's trying that route. It's disregarding the total entity. If you can stand ten feet away from a mirror and see NECKTIE, go and change it. But that's applicable to a man of any size too. Anything that's too distracting—texture, color, pattern, shape—quite simply is wrong.

"A person who is well-dressed—when all the parts fit—is someone you look at but never say, 'Hey, look at the way that tie goes with that shirt with that jacket.' No one should look like a window display in a men's store. Dressing requires credibility. There's a very fine line between expression and ostentation or exhibitionism."

PART 2

THE LOOKS
DISCOVERING YOURSELF

Every outfit you wear is seen in a setting. The majority of men worry most about what to wear in their working environment.

Unfortunately, that's also what worries too many employers.

Morally indefensible, dress codes, whether written or unspoken, are devised by small minds in big rooms. Categorizing individuals by dress transforms clothing into a segregationist tool.

Consider the implications of the corporate image. One's position in the hierarchy is supposedly not only reflected, but announced, by the way one dresses. Employees are reduced to walking sandwich boards advertising their status. Accountants, a myopic flock according to myth, are assigned the plummage of dreary, ill-fitting suits. Creative birds are expected to be peacocks, since those at the top have resolved that arty fellows are too flighty to wing their way to the presidency; let them strut, they can't ruffle any important feathers. Corporate vice presidents must glide along in their carefully tailored suits without any suggestion of preening. The ground-level boys in the mail room can display themselves as they will, dodos that they are thought to be.

Heaven help the corporation if anyone attempts to break the mold. No doubt the superstructure would collapse if an accountant switched attire with an art director and pored over his ledgers in a leather blazer.

Pigeonholing all accountants, all art directors, all corporate vice presidents is fraudulent. But isn't that the guano we're forced to swallow if we accept the premise that men should dress to express their positions in life? No, not life. Their positions in the corporate nest, a predatory place. And how dare anyone dismiss mail boys as creatures beneath contempt? There are more mail boys than chairmen of the board.

Corporate dress codes, reprehensible as they are, have their counterparts outside the working environment as well. Their mentality invades society at large. We all make assumptions about others based on what they wear, often making gross errors in judgment. No one can claim the right to write someone off because of his dress. Conversely, we're fools if we grant indiscriminate favor simply because we like the way someone looks. Appearances can deceive, otherwise undercover agents would all be unemployed. We owe it to others and ourselves to scratch beneath the surface. And that includes scratching superficial thinking.

Back to the corporate image.

If you're an accountant and enjoy wearing rumpled suits, no problem. Lean back and join in the hearty laughter accompanying accountant jokes. But should a fellow accountant bedeck himself in a fringed vest and cowboy boots, give the guy a break. Certainly the corporation won't. No wonder lots of guys opt for being human clothes racks, permitting others to toss garments on their outstretched limbs. It's safer that way.

But it isn't. When we allow ourselves to seem stereotypes, we're prey to stereotypic thinking. When we think that it's advisable, let alone possible, to dress to the expectations of others, we overlook the fact that those others can, and often will, read us all wrong regardless. Reputable clairvoyants have spotty records, so how can we expect to read petty minds with much accuracy? Even pleasing some of the people some of the time is a sporadic occurrence. Pleasing yourself is easier, since you know what you want. Or should. If you don't, find out. Then you'll experience that lift of doing yourself proud.

If the foregoing sounds a bit idealistic, it may well be. Of course, everyone must make some clothing concessions. *Some.* If you are expected to wear a suit within a specific setting, you probably will. Or a sport jacket. But the style of the suit or jacket, its cut and color, what accessories to wear with it—these choices are your own. When stepping out casually, you'll still most likely want to fit in, at least roughly, with the game plan. But the outcome needn't be fixed.

Dressing to the expectations of others interferes with a lot of your fun, especially when your decision to try is made negatively. Choosing any outfit becomes a worrisome hassle when you're clutched wondering if your efforts will be good enough. When you approve of what you're wearing, you're forearmed with self-confidence, a self-confidence you'll project to those around you. That air will lend credence to your whole being, clothes included.

Tell yourself that you can choose from all the clothing styles available. You've got the guts and the charisma to carry it off. Or at least you're willing to try. You may end up wearing just what you have in your wardrobe today. But maybe you won't. Only after blazing the trail can you discover if the destination is worth reaching. But any surveying will make you more surefooted.

Chapter

SUITING YOURSELF

*Undoubtedly menswear will continue
in its freer evolution.*

STRIKING OUT

Man does not live by vested suit alone.

For the majority of men, wearing suits and ties is not one of life's greater pleasures. Don't most guys yearn for a string of days when they can go grubby?

Perhaps one reason wearing suits can be such a drudge is due to all the societal injunctions about image and acceptability.

"I wonder if a lot of men's insecurity about dressing isn't based on corporation dressing, inasmuch as you have to really and truly dress in a way that does not detract from your immediate superior," ponders Bill Blass. "I don't suppose there's a city in the world more interesting in this respect than Detroit. Talk about corporation dressing, baby. You wouldn't dare wear a blue shirt if your immediate superior only wore white.

"It has always bothered me," he continues, "because I've never seen the reason for it, that a doctor—God knows they don't make house calls anymore—should wear enormously conservative, dour clothes that only they and lawyers seem to wear. Why is it that only photographers and writers and artists can wear so-called weekend

clothes during the week to do their business?"

Why indeed? The only way dressing right can be personally rewarding is if it becomes personal. Period.

Ronald Kolodzie correctly points out, "Men shouldn't be made to feel that clothing themselves has to be such an important decision. So somebody makes a mistake. I've worn some things that by the time I got to the office I thought, 'God!' Anyway, men aren't going to be that outrageous. Working with suits or sport jackets and shirts and ties, how big a mistake can someone make? Unless he's wearing patchwork-quilted pants. You have to make the mistakes and keep trying combinations to get an answer to what works for you."

Although suit styles (called "models" by the clothing trade) change season by season, the modifications are seldom dramatic, and the basic elements of a suit remain pretty much the same. As Bill Kaiserman explains, "In men's fashion, it's very rare that you can create a new model altogether, or a new shape that applies. A woman's body, because of the curves, has no restrictions about the types of shapes—narrow, big, flowing or tailored—that can be worn on it. A man's chest being flatter and his waist being wider means his

body cannot take certain extreme treatments. Oh, you can try. But since man represents a more classic being, the more classic he looks, the better he looks."

MOVING ALONG

Proof that the movement of menswear has been toward more relaxation and greater freedom is that what today is considered the epitome of formal attire—top hat and tails—was worn in the mid-18th century for horseback riding. A hundred years later tails had climbed the social ladder and something new was needed to separate the gentleman's formal wardrobe from his sporting attire. That void was filled with a so-called lounge suit, the precursor to today's traditional suits. Sport jackets were developed for playing and spectating when lounge suits gained respectability and stopped passing themselves off as sportswear. By the latter 70s, sport coats were accepted, if begrudgingly, as serious businesswear by most companies. Thus, although we refer to suits as businesswear, sport jackets and slacks now occupy some of that same territory, especially since the emergence of the non-suit-looking suit.

Menswear does evolve, and will continue to do so. Sometimes dressing moves toward more polarized looks; sometimes it heads toward more similarity among looks. Paradoxically, right now men's wearables are undergoing both processes simultaneously. On the one hand, the distinctions between conventional suit styles—the American cut, the British cut and the European cut—are blurring into a certain homogenization. But also gaining in momentum is an entirely new, polarized mode of dressing that might be termed the My-Own-Turf style. It has drawn eclectically from various sources and inspirations. It has been called an "attitudinal" look, which is as good an adjective as any, if not particularly descriptive.

In relative terms, My-Own-Turf outfits are less constricted by convention than the American, British or European styles which have formed the basis for the suit vocabulary for a number of years.

Décontracté, a term from the French without a literal translation applicable to clothing, is one approach to this more polarized clothing expression. The word doesn't exactly mean unconstructed or deconstructed, but garments in this vein are relaxed in fabrication and outline. The clothing's state of mind—its attitude—is flexible; the cloth-

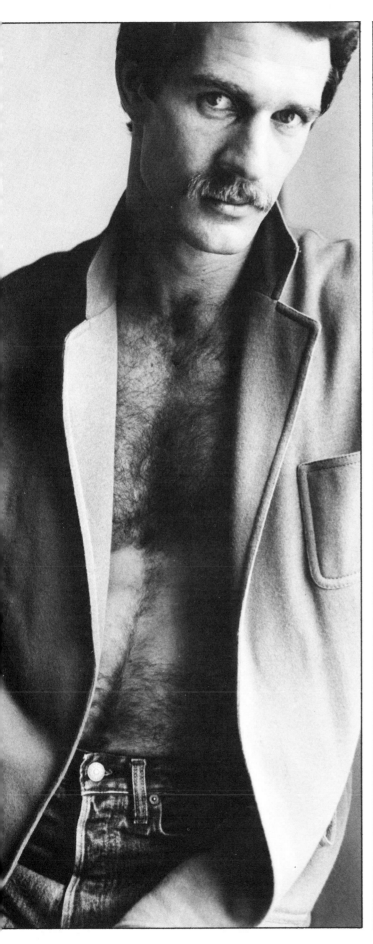

ing's state of body—the invisible inner construction customarily used to shape tailored clothing—is absent altogether or decidedly on the soft side, as opposed to "hard" tailoring. Linings and padding are often eliminated, so that jackets may drape like shirts. Proportions are often over-sized, particularly at the top, and individual items are often layered. The pieces commonly come in non-matching fabrics with strong textural contrast. Natural fibers and colors contribute largely to the look.

Décontracté outfits, some commentators have analyzed, represent "shabby chic" and/or "purposeful disarray." American designer Bert Pulitzer, who doesn't see this mode of dressing as all that innovative, remarks, "The look was invented years ago by little old men sitting on park benches."

But *décontracté* is only one way of taking a definitive step away from the norm. The My-Own-Turf syndrome encompasses any manner of dressing that causes controversy, perhaps even consternation and alarm. Initially the majority will always see any My-Own-Turf look as a personal affront. After a while, when more than a few pick up on any new look or way of dressing, a trend is born. Whether a trend will achieve mass acceptance is seldom apparent at its inception.

Undoubtedly menswear in general will continue in its "freer" evolution. The arc of history proves that. How that freedom will be expressed is unclear. Examining men's suits won't uncloud the crystal ball, since the future of men's clothing will emanate from sportswear, a subject discussed in the next chapter. Meanwhile, dealing with today and an immediate tomorrow, let's examine suits (sport jackets too) in their current light.

NATIONAL ORIGINS

Men's suits do not come in endless array.

True, fabrics, colors, textures and patterns change, as do some of the details. Nonetheless, conventional suits—those we think of when we hear the phrase "business suit," ignoring the fact that the majority of men don't wear suits while going about the business of earning their livings—are variations on three themes: American, British and European.

Today, the terminology survives, although the ancestry isn't always readily clear or even necessarily legitimate. During the mid-70s, the ubiquitous suit style worn by many American men was in the European look—not in the "American" style at all. Within each category, styles range from conservative to liberal. And, of course, the borderlines separating the categories are often hazy.

Luciano Franzoni, the Italian-born designer for Hart Schaffner & Marx, American's menswear giant, explains that the basis of the three major suit influences is the *silhouette,* the term referring to the outline or "cut" of a suit. He also points out that the stereotypic descriptions apply more to styles worn in the early- to mid-70s than to those worn by the fashionable today.

AMERICAN CUT

"The American silhouette is fuller in the body of the jacket than the other styles," Franzoni notes. "There is less shape. The armholes tend to be lower. The shoulders are tailored, not naturally soft as in the British or Ivy styles. (Some people think of Ivy League as pure American. I don't. Ivy is a blend of American and British.)

"The true American shoulder looks very much

like a natural shoulder (which means it has little or no padding), but it really has been carefully tailored to add some dimension to the shoulders without building them up, as opposed to the built-up, roped European shoulder.

"The jacket is usually center vented," Franzoni goes on, "but not very deeply. Of course, British and European jackets can be center vented too. We're talking about the most characteristic aspects.

"Generally, the trousers on a suit in the American style are not cuffed, I suppose because American men don't seem to like cuffs very much. The vest is common to all styles."

BRITISH CUT

Franzoni tackles the fundamental elements of this world-traveled look. "Usually both American and British jackets have notched lapels, but British lapels are often wider. Also, the British jacket tends to be a little longer and a little closer to the body. More shaped, it traditionally has side vents.

"A typical touch is hacking pockets that most

often are flapped, plus a ticket or change pocket, instead of straight flap pockets very often found on American styles. Patch pockets are more American too, but are seen on British cuts.

"Cuffed trousers, with their country gentlemanly connotation, aren't obligatory, but they're more associated with the British look than uncuffed trousers.

"Nubby wools and tweeds can be cut in any style but often suggest the British look."

EUROPEAN CUT

"European suits, or what we *think of* as having European looks, have gotten away from that very, very shaped silhouette," the designer comments, "but we still think of European styling, as it relates to America, as distinguished by greater waist suppression, wider lapels and higher armholes. As is the case with American and British styles, European jackets may come in either single- or double-breasted models, double-breasted being thought the dressier. European jackets are more likely to be nonvented.

"The European man wears his trousers some-

what longer. Wait. I hate generalizations, although I'm generalizing," Franzoni exclaims. "*Some* European men wear their pants longer than *some* American or British men. Anyway, longer pants *may* be tailored to slant, so the length is longer where the trousers touch the heel of the shoe in back. That slant is very difficult to achieve with cuffs, so the so-called European or Italian man seldom wears cuffs."

PIECING TOGETHER

Whatever terminology may be applied to categorize clothing, we are moving toward a more international style.

Franzoni explains which components in each style *customarily* speak the same language. But you can always choose to be multilingual.

"There are truly no dictates other than personal taste," he remarks. "Still, a man should think about what's good for him. A tie with a large knot is bad for someone whose stature is small. A shortish spread collar might be fine with an American or British suit, but not with a double-breasted style; the proportions would be off. If a button-down collar is deep enough, theoretically it would be in the right proportion to be worn with a single-breasted European suit, but traditionally the look would be wrong.

"Ties are the most flexible part of a wardrobe, certainly much more so than shirts. But if a man avoids extremes—say he knots his ties in the usual four-in-hand manner, producing a moderate knot, and supposing he wears shirt collars that are neither extremely short nor long, and not too widely spread either—keeping these components mostly standard, then they will be appropriate for American, British or European suits."

On specifics as they relate to particular silhouettes or not, Franzoni sets forth the following guidelines.

SHIRTS

"Whatever the shirt style, you should see a little of the cuff below the jacket sleeves if you wear long-sleeve shirts. And, by all means, wear long-sleeve shirts with suits. Short collars, or rounded collars, are better with the narrower lapels of American suits. Longer collars are better with wider lapels, with traditional British or European styles. But, to repeat, if the collars or the lapels are not extreme—and today's menswear is pretty much in a classic mood—it makes very little difference what shirt style is worn. In general, British and American styling are probably more compatible than American and European."

TIES

"Right now, the tendency is toward the narrower tie, which also means shorter, smaller shirt collars. Especially in Europe, some young men are purposefully wearing their ties very short. It's a look. Who can say it's wrong? I personally think that the windsor knot looks out of date. Certainly, even British men no longer wear it. Of course, if a man is six-foot-five and weighs 225 pounds, he can carry off big tie knots. I like sportier ties with sportier fabrics. The more texture, the sportier. But what is more British than a silk regimental tie with tweeds? If it looks and feels good, wear it."

ASCOTS

This style of neckwear is traditionally not worn with fine tailored suits, Franzoni advises, but he believes ascots are appropriate with British country suits (minus their vests) and any style blazer. "I personally like ascots because, when you're a certain age, and if you have a neck that looks like a turtle's, then you should wear something to cover it—whether it's a turtleneck, ascot or scarf."

POCKET SQUARES

The designer raises his eyebrows. "As long as the square doesn't look painted above the pocket, fine. I detest that little line of white peeking out. Pocket squares, which have always been more widely worn by Continental than American or even British males, mustn't look too artificial. They're difficult to wear with very wide lapels; they look squashed in."

SHOES

"With trim silhouettes—and American, British and European suits are all trimming their lapels and proportions—shoes should be soft and lightweight, with almost no soles. Of course, sturdier

fabrics—tweeds and woolens, associated with the British style as we know it—can be worn with sturdier shoes. Slip-ons with tassels also look very good with the British look. For the American silhouette, plain slip-ons are fine. I also like lightweight but classic wingtips, a dressier style."

HATS

"Perhaps the United States is the only country in the western world where hats are still worn by men. Nobody in America turns in surprise seeing a man wearing an antique on his head. In hats, as in all clothing, harmony counts. A feather band is more casual than a silk ribbon. Brims relate to lapel widths. Narrower lapels, narrower brims."

In summary, while noting that "There must be a link between all the components," Franzoni cautions against becoming compulsive about matching the pieces. "I dislike anything that smacks of putting a man in a slot, into a uniform. Adaptable men—and there are more and more—can wear a European style one day, a contemporary American look the next, without feeling strange."

At this point in menswear's evolution, style distinctions are mainly arbitrary. Seeking to present a totally consistent stylistic facade can be a misguided effort, since national clothing styles aren't that easy to discern one from each other and are always reinterpreted when transplanted. Within each category, although the conventional components of each will presumably be in the right approximate proportion to be worn with each other, they may not work together correctly in terms of your body proportions. For example, a suit in the would-be European manner theoretically calls for a longer, more widely spreading collar, but if you have a thick, squat neck, you should be wearing a shorter collar with a narrower spread. Stylistic compatibility, then, is incompatible with your frame's clothing requirements once you select that type of European suit. Better to break consistency within a style or look than to break down your personal presentation. So, the following more elaborate compilation of what items most characteristically comprise the three looks should be viewed with a cynical eye. Staying within national boundaries may not be your passport to dressing right.

AMERICAN STYLE

SUITS. Most often single-breasted. Double-breasted are considered dressier. Little or no shape to the jacket. Predominantly notched lapels. Trousers, usually with plain fronts and no cuffs, often worn relatively short. Colors most commonly used are navy, camel and gray. Brown, though widespread, is more associated with the British style. Fabrics often smoothly textured. Hopsackings too. Patterning, minimal; conventional stripes, checks or plaids.

SPORT JACKETS. Blazers are very popular. Wider ranges of colors, including reds and other brights. More texture too, with tweeds and herringbones, but not extremely fuzzy or nubby. Man-made suedes. Patterns of mid-scale, except for larger, bolder plaids.

VESTS. When worn, usually matching suit or sport jacket. Dark or red with plaid jackets; tartan plaids with blazers and some tweeds. Those of corduroy or suede are less widely worn. Classic sweater vests—sleeveless V-necks and cable cardigans.

DRESS SHIRTS. Button-downs; standard collars with moderate length and spread; tab collars. White and light blue oxford cloth, other pastel shades. Stripes a favored pattern.

NECKWEAR. Ties of moderate width. Silks and knits are most pervasive. Great variety in colors and patterns. Strong on stripes and foulard-type prints.

SHOES. Wingtips and other conservative lace-ups. Slip-ons with tassels. Black, brown or Cordovan leathers.

SOCKS. Solids, heathers, ribs, argyles.

OUTERWEAR. Trench coats. Polo coats. Topcoats, single- or double-breasted, with fly fronts and notched lapels. Navy, black, gray or camel. Solids, herringbones, subtle tweeds and checks. Length just below the knees.

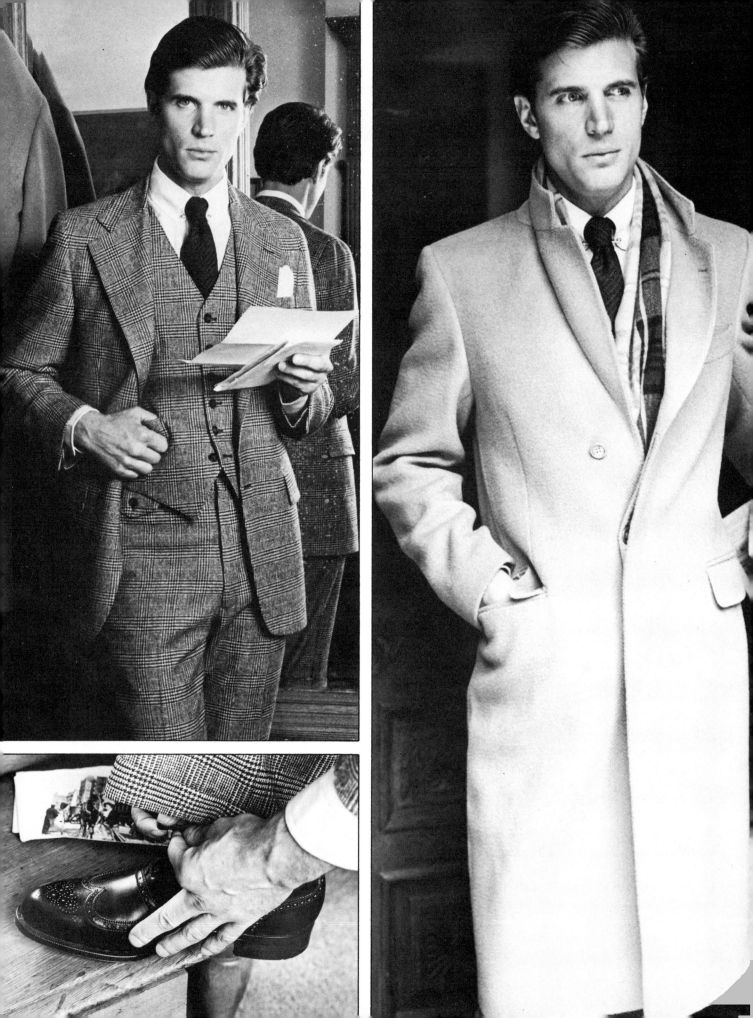

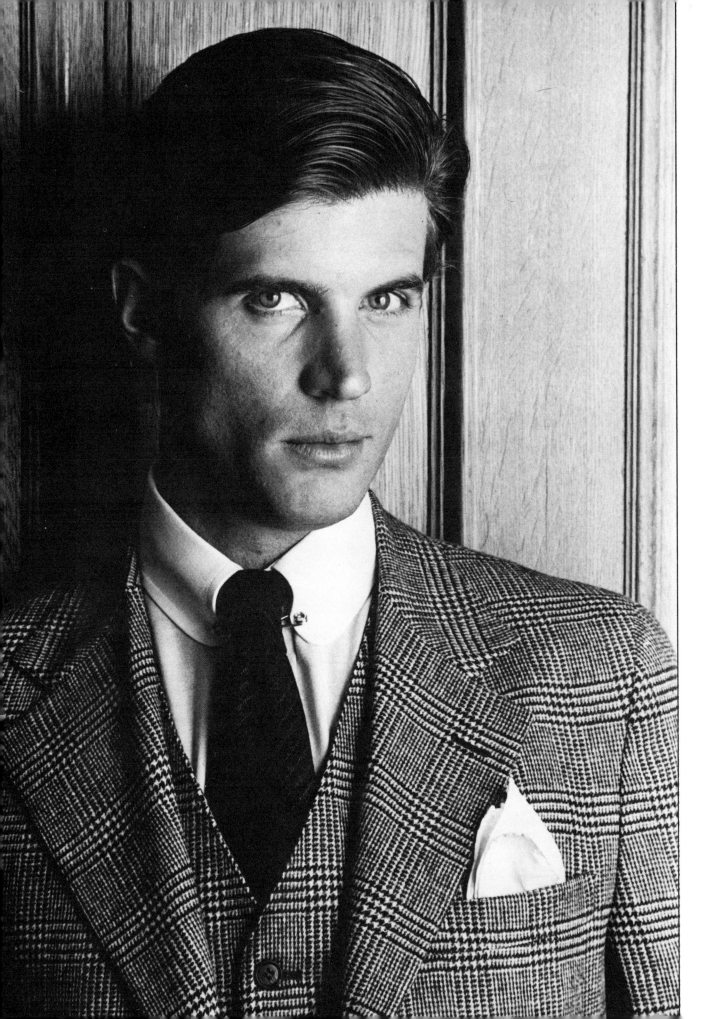

BRITISH STYLE

SUITS. More likely to be double-breasted than American styles. Commonly more shaped, longer, with wider lapels. Trousers more likely to be pleated and cuffed, though plain fronts and no cuffs remain the norm in each category. Colors most commonly used are browns, earth tones, grays, plus the ubiquitous blues. In finely tailored suits, smooth fabrics and flannels; textured cheviots not uncommon. So-called country suits in stronger textures; herringbones and tweeds and twills. More pronounced patterning, with chalk stripes, district checks and glen plaids with a wider variety of earth and foliage colors, including rusts and maroons and numerous blendings.

SPORT JACKETS. More varied silhouettes than the boxier, looser American styles. Hacking, norfolk and manor models. Sometimes back- or fully-belted. More overall detailing, with pocket treatments more pronounced. Touches such as throat latches, wind tabs, elbow and gun patches

may be present. Shetlands and cashmeres. Very textured fabrics. Patterns from small pin checks to exaggerated plaids. Blended colors even when in contrasting hues.

VESTS. Widely used, whether matching, coordinating or contrasting.

DRESS SHIRTS. Moderate collars. Contrast collars more likely. Many different stripings; tattersalls and checks. Fine cottons.

NECKWEAR. Typically, clubs and regimental stripes. Small, neat patterns. Also, homespuns. Bow ties more frequently seen than with any other style. Per usual, neckwear the most versatile category, with greatest variety of color, texture and pattern. Ascots very British.

SHOES. Oxfords, brogues, kilties. All leathers and suedes. Lace-ups more prevalent than slip-ons. "Sensible" shoes.

SOCKS. Marled tones. Textural patterns. Cables. Solids and heathers. Argyles.

OUTERWEAR. Burberry trenches. British warms. Balmacaans. Chesterfields. In meltons and tweeds and twills. Longer than American styles, often fuller in the body.

EUROPEAN STYLE

SUITS. More severely styled, often with built-up, roped shoulders. Peaked lapels not obligatory but more prominent. Nonvented. Some double-breasted models cut for lower-button fastening with sloping, low closure. Understated pocket treatments. Trousers may or may not be pleated; seldom cuffed. Wide range of colors: black, creams, greens, browns and grays. Blues, of course. Some lighter-weight, smoothish fabrics; gabardines, mohairs, sharkskins. Raw silks and other nubby naturals. Also, saxonies and various more complicated weaves, though not in British feel. Small, even delicate, pattern effects often evident in the weaves and textures. Pattern combinations, such as chalk and pencil stripes together.

SPORT JACKETS. On the dressier side. Not heavily into tweeds or plaids. More discreet patterns. Minimal extraneous details, although lapels may be stitched.

VESTS. Often with fewer buttons and a deeper V. Some have lapels. More light-dark contrasts than in the other styles. More textural contrast too.

DRESS SHIRTS. Longer collars, wider spread. High, rounded collars too. Some contrast collars and cuffs. White-on-whites, satin stripes. Ecru and off-white as well as pure white or deeper tones in definite colors. Combinations of stripes, neat patterns. Finer weaves. Some fly and French fronts.

NECKWEAR. Silks and silk knits. Wider widths. Many solid colors, but a variety of patterns as well. Vast choice. Scarf treatments on sportier outfits.

SHOES. Very lightweight. Narrower toes. Cap toes. Seamless lace-ups. Elegant slip-ons. Less grain to the shinier leathers.

SOCKS. Lighter in weight, finer. Dark colors. Thick and thin ribs. Diamond self-patterns. Clock-stitching motifs.

OUTERWEAR. Generally more shaped. Dark chesterfields. Trim topcoats. Wrap coats, lodens and furs. Period-inspired coats with larger collars, deeper vents and more flare. Longest in length, sometimes below mid-calf. Hand and shoulder bags accompany.

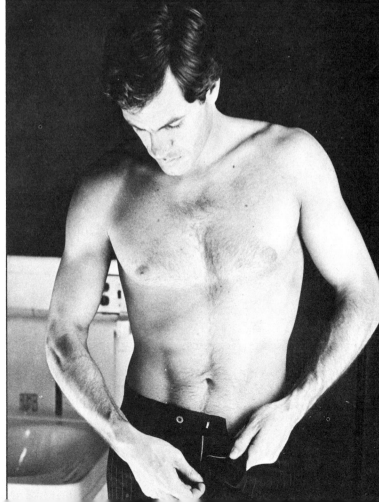

To say it one more time: the foregoing typify the standard, time-accepted ingredients in the three national recipes for conventional suit fare. But standardized dressing always reflects where clothing has been, not where it is and *definitely* not where it is going. The new hasn't been slotted yet.

Shawl collars, which for years had been found only on sweaters and tuxedos, were reintroduced to American men at the end of the 70s in suit and sport jacket lapels by name designers. Which style do shawl lapels fit into? None of the above, really. Maybe in the catchall clothes hamper of My-Own-Turf? Yes, in that shawl lapels are hardly into the mainstream yet. And may never be. But, no, they don't fit in if My-Own-Turf is limited to the soft, *décontracté* alternate mode of dressing. Does slotting everything and everybody down to the smallest detail really matter?

SOFT TOUCH

The *décontracté* idiom is out to change the accent of American menswear with its new body language.

One of its proponents is Alan Flusser, a behind-the-scenes menswear designer who stepped forward in the middle 70s. Having styled Pierre Cardin's popularly-priced American sportswear, he also began designing his own tailored clothing, the former much imbued with the *décontracté* spirit, the latter very formally, though softly, tailored.

Flusser, who clothes himself in the gentlemanly Saville Row tradition of custom-made suits of his creating, remarks, "At this time you can't really impose fashion. The look is very eclectic. There are guys who are so tied into fitted, shaped clothing that they can't make the transition into pleated pants, for example, that don't really fit snugly and that don't give these men, psychologically, a kind of sexual feeling.

"But a shaped, highly fitted suit can be boring," he comments. "You can't layer it. It's hard to work with. The majority of Americans—the world, for that matter—is still into fitted clothing, clothes that fit tight.

"If you're confident enough about your own physique, confident enough to wear clothing that drapes on, not conforms to, the body, then wearing softer clothes affords you a certain amount of freedom within clothes. A sensuality as opposed to overt sexuality. Then you can walk and move the

way you want without your suit going right along with you like cardboard.

"Ultimately, soft garments require a person to stamp his own personality on them. That comes from the way that they are worn. If you wear a *décontracté* jacket like a conventional sport jacket, it isn't fashion. But if you slouch it up a bit, push up the sleeves, plunge your hands deeply into the jacket pockets and flip up the collar, then it's high fashion."

Décontracté, like any clothing innovation, will continue modifying itself or will disappear. The latter is unlikely. Currently the style is considered more a sportswear than a suit look. But that's hair-splitting, the overreaction of the confused majority who don't fathom its implications—that men's suits needn't be an uptight business. *Décontracté* is an option.

So is any My-Own-Turf variation from the establishment norm. If fashion is an attitude, then attitudinal clothing is what you make of it.

WISE CHOICE

"Any given person could look good in any type of silhouette, provided that the designer was able to fit him personally." So says Bill Kaiserman. And, considering his next statement, his words are not reassuring: "In ready-to-wear, we can't do that."

Continuing frankly, Kaiserman says, "I think that the tall, athletically-built or slim man can wear clothing more easily than anyone else. I always keep this well-proportioned guy in mind to achieve the ultimate looks. I realize from there that men go in degrees away from the ultimate, but I start with one fabulous look on that one fabulous person. When a design looks perfect on him, then I figure that it won't look so bad when it trickles down to the worst. But if it doesn't look perfect on the best-proportioned person, forget it, because then it's not going to look good on anyone."

Here we are, faced with our own bodies again, not perfection.

Suits can be selected according to the Ideal Norm. (A rundown of somatotypic considerations for all body types and all apparel items is compiled in the "Body Works" section.) If you do so, don't become imprisoned by it. The Ideal Norm is a tool to use if you find it helpful. Certainly somatotypic advice is not meant as an ironclad commandment. These guidelines were devised as starting points for experimentation.

We mostly think about developing a personal style. The goal is to develop our own best look or looks. But Ronald Kolodzie points out how this concept—My Best Look—can be perilous.

"Sometimes men get cemented into a look," he remarks. "It may be a look they wore in college, because that's when they really did look best. But in their forties that collegiate look is ridiculous on them. Their bodies and lives have changed, but their clothes haven't. Or, when they are mature, men may settle on another My Best Look. And they won't deviate from it, even though new looks have been introduced that weren't around when they made their decisions. Decisions, like rules, don't hold forever. Or shouldn't. Some men are so stubborn you have to take them by the shoulders to get them to try any goddam new thing on."

Even though you've been advised not to follow fashion blindly, that doesn't mean that you should wear blinders. Nor does it mean you should follow

the Ideal Norm blindly either. Remember, the Ideal Norm deals with *generalized* proportions. The suggestion for the stringy ectomorph, for example, is to stick to moderate lapels, on the supposition that wide lapels will overpower his chest and emphasize the narrowness of his shoulders, whereas skimpy lapels with their more linear lines will only reinforce his body's linearity. However, the descriptions wide, moderate and narrow lapels are relative to the styles around. During the 50s, "moderate" lapels were, to today's eye, very narrow indeed. On the other hand, today's wide lapels would have been considered moderate only several years ago, when WIDE lapels were enjoying a heyday.

Fashion moves in cycles. To a certain degree, you can't avoid being influenced by it. When your wardrobe needs replenishing, you select from what's available, right? And what's available, offered in a small to large range, always reflects what is considered currently fashionable. The Ideal Norm, theoretically timeless, is affected by the times. It can't exist in a vacuum. And neither should you.

Developing a personal style, then, revolves around three awarenesses. The awareness that clothing is constantly evolving and, consequently, that you shouldn't automatically damn any look without at least first giving it the benefit of the doubt; we can be too slow in our adaptation to change. Second, the awareness that your body proportions can be affected by what you wear but that the guidelines of the Ideal Norm should encourage, not inhibit, experimentation; we can get locked into a look prematurely. And, third, the related awareness that no clothing decisions are final: life goes on no matter how we dress ourselves. We might as well enjoy clothes. They are a continuing aspect of living freely.

How *do* you choose a personal style?

First, by deciding what clothes you like, the ones that make you feel good. That's right, *you*. Not the corporation. Not your mate. Not the fashion columnists. *You*. If you like several different looks, probably your personal style should be eclectic.

Then, after deciding what clothing style(s) you like, go to a men's store and try on as many of those outfits as the clerk's patience will allow. Don't say you haven't got the time. Find the time. Then, go to another store. This time try on styles you're not positive that you like. *Find the time*. Resolve to hit as many stores as possible, alternating between the likes and the unsures, for up to a month, without making a purchase. Well, maybe a tie. Purposefully try on different colors and patterns. During this time, keep your eyes open to somatotypic considerations: judge the differences. Allow some passage of time before trying the same outfits on twice. The second time around, be more watchful with the unsures. Styles you previously were uncertain about may now have grown on you. Finally, recognize that enough is enough. Sooner or later you will have to decide on your personal style. *You*.

In other words, get involved. A personal style doesn't drop like manna from heaven.

Chapter

5

LIBERATING YOURSELF

*Wearing casual clothing is a personal matter
where we present ourselves as free agents.*

TURN ONS

Suits aren't sexy. Or seldom are.

Sportswear is sexy. Or can be.

One of the prime reasons for dressing is to get undressed.

Wearing suits represents a nod to conventional mores, dressing as others expect us to for particular occasions. Wearing casual clothing, commonly called sportswear, is a personal matter where we present ourselves as free agents, liberated from any associations with professional status. Nine to five, we're lawyers, farmers, opera singers, television repairmen, account executives, whatever. Off duty is when we select clothes to communicate a driving obsession or a whimsical fancy, a time when we want to project as much magnetism as we can muster.

"Maybe it's the disco mentality. Or because of women's liberation," muses Egon Von Furstenberg. "I think that we are all more aware that women are looking at men sexually. Women are very practical now. They want to get what they want. For years, millions of women never came. Woman was an object, the man came in, in-out, in-out, and then good-bye. Now, if she's not happy,

she's going to look next door. So a man tries to look the best that he can. Before she wouldn't even dare look at him. It used to be unethical for a woman to look up when a handsome man walked into a restaurant.

"More and more men are dressing to look sexy," Von Furstenberg continues. "Because sex, as it's finally opened, is not any more a sin. People want a sexy look, not a chic look. Imagine somebody who goes to the gym—and a lot of guys go—and then he goes out on his Friday or his Saturday night with a classic suit on. People might say, 'My god, he's put together.' But they won't want to get into his pants.''

Robert Stock, the sportswear designer whose name precedes "for Country Roads," also picks up on the sexual nature of clothing.

"The first time people meet, right after you first come eye to eye with someone, you look to see what he's wearing. You don't know whether he's smart, but you know whether he looks sexy. Age in sportswear usually looks good, because it has an air of sophistication about it, an air of having been around. It's like breaking in a pair of jeans. They look better a year later because they have a whole attitude about them. They're worn-in, they fit

tight, and your ass fits in right. The same also applies with a rugged flannel shirt after repeated wearings. Then the body becomes more important than the design of the shirt."

Some body-consciousness is always integral to clothes appearing sexual. Bill Kaiserman thinks contrast is at the core. "Take two extremes. A pair of skin-tight jeans with a hugging T-shirt and a big shirt with a pair of loose, sloppy pants. A tight pair of jeans and the T-shirt are sexy, but more sexy when you throw a big sweater over them. A big, loose pair of pants and a big top can be quite sexy when you throw on a great big belt right around the waist to bring it all in. Sexy is not in revealing anything. It's in the movement, so that you're aware of all these different parts of the body."

"Any outfit can look sexy if it's worn right," suggests Ronald Kolodzie. "Big tops can look sexy and hot by rolling up the sleeves and showing some chest. What you feel like is what you are. How you see yourself doesn't *really* change your physical structure, but in a sense it does. Most people don't realize how good, how sexy, they can look. They get confused about their possibilities, saying, 'Oh, I can't wear that, I'd look silly.' For people to go through life thinking that they are less

than perfect, putting a mental clamp on themselves, is such a shame. As opposed to people I know who are tiny, or all kinds of shapes, who throw together all kinds of looks. They just make themselves look fabulous."

Whether we dress to undress or not—a major issue for us personally—is not a central issue in dressing right. Even if you're celibate (why? *why?*), you have more room to play round in sportswear than tailored clothing. Our workday wardrobes are probably fairly structured, with only variations on a theme, but our casual wardrobes are open to a tempo-changing world of possibilities and roles.

In sportswear, you're always granted more license. The colors can be bolder and brighter, the patterns more freewheeling, the shapes novel. Someone who might balk seeing a man wearing a magenta and shocking pink paisley three-piece suit could pass the same guy in a magenta and shocking pink short-sleeve shirt without a second glance.

Chip Tolbert recommends that men who are reticent about taking adventurous strides in serious clothing start at a crawl with sportswear. "Sportswear can be an area of experimentation,"

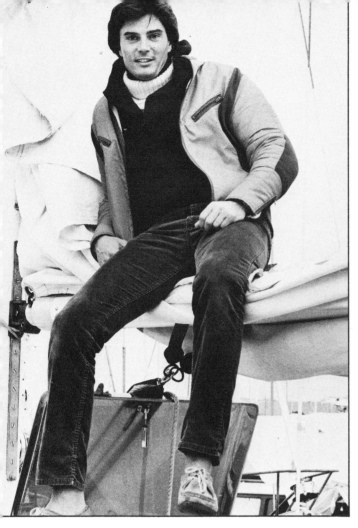

Tolbert says. "A man who's unsure of mixing color, texture and pattern can get away with more in sportswear, going into training before challenging the main event, his business wardrobe. Once a man gets into experimentation, it's like eating peanuts."

Alan Flusser points out, "Strictly speaking, there are rules of proportion that should apply to all dressing. However, if the garment looks good, but not on you, what's the point? One plus in sportswear is that you have much more room to maneuver in. It doesn't matter so much if a jacket is 31- or 32-inches long, because if the jacket is worn in a loose way, it doesn't have to finish at a specific point as a suit jacket does."

Although the concept of the Ideal Norm still applies to sportswear, the application, like the garments, is looser. On the other hand, when aiming for hard-core body-consciousness, if you're not a well-endowed mesomorph, you might want to watch somatotypic guidelines even more carefully. Tough to know. Some badly-proportioned (by objective standards) men can project more appeal than perfectly-chiseled types who are as cold as statuary. Sexy is what works for whom you're after.

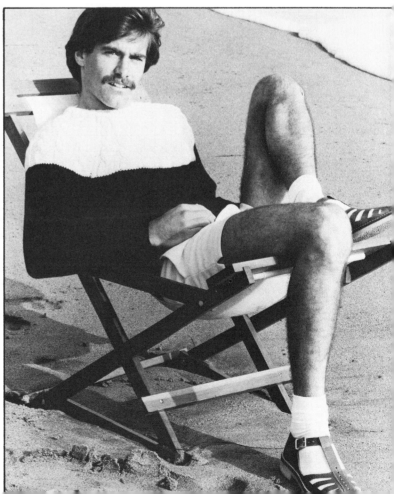

ACTIVE SPORTS INFLUENCE

Everybody's playing the game.

Tenniswear is one of the more obvious examples. Once tennis was a game of gentility, so elitist that during the 30s only traditional white garb was allowed on country club clay. With the tennis explosion among people of all incomes, color became the order of the court. Familiar placket-front knit shirts gave way to now-familiar ring necks and V-necks and other interpretations. White flannel slacks, first *de rigeur,* were replaced by various shorts or cut-off jeans. Tennis sneakers came into their own as a whole new footloose shoe category. Today, tennis clothes are as much street as sport fashion.

On the courts, all-whites aren't just snobby. White reflects more sunlight than other colors, and is thus cooler when the game's pace becomes heated. As off-the-court fashion, a classic white tennis shirt isn't always all that hot a choice. Though crisp, pure white draws attention to itself. Dark and mid-tones would be better on someone with a hefty torso or midsection that requires no additional emphasis. In less conventional styling, round-neck tennis shirts without collars and plackets are better for short men; both details complicate the top of the chest area, breaking up the vertical line of the body when spatial expansion is desired.

Golf is another sporty source of casual attire. The game originated in Scotland, and Scottish knickers were the rage in the 20s and 30s. Today, golf enthusiasts might think a golfer in knickers birdie-brained, but knickers can be fun in an off-beat way. While they will never be universally accepted, knickers prove how the active sports influence has a way of shedding its previous associations and becoming a more generalized, casual look.

More in the sportswear mainstream for casual attire are golf shirts, cardigan sweaters and golf jackets, which have likewise lost many of their links to the links and have become familiar weekend garments for many men in their own backyards. Again, the point is that sport clothing is becoming more universal, less connected to the original action. However, the typical golf cardigan is less flattering to a stringy ectomorph than a typical argyle V-neck.

In this sporty vein, skiwear became influential in menswear after World War I. Bulky, colorful sweaters, hooded jackets and other ski accoutrements have sped off the slopes to give comfort to city dwellers.

The principle for maintaining body heat in skiwear is based on layering. Air captured between the layers insulates the person within against the cold. Sweaters and down-filled vests do their parts.

For the sport, voluminous parkas and volumes of garments under them make perfect sense. On the Y-shaped or barrel-chested man on the street, this layered approach is misdirected; his proportions would rival King Kong's.

Football, baseball, basketball, rugby and soccer have all likewise provided designers with inspirations. The outfits are, by connotation if not by actual wearing, more body-conscious than tailored ensembles. And there is more room for humor...baseball jackets and ties, jogging pants with tuxedo jackets.

In short, just as today's formalwear was once considered sportswear, athletic influences have supported new looks in menswear for years. It is entirely possible that today's sportswear will be translated and reinterpreted into tomorrow's serious businesswear. Certainly history provides the precedent.

Meanwhile, various philosophies exist about the active sports influence. Egon Von Furstenberg says, "Sportswear is more difficult to put together than tailored clothing, much more. Whatever is related to active sportswear looks good because it's practical, but only if it's real. When you get into very, very fancy and too fashion-conscious sportswear, often you make mistakes. A sweatshirt should look like a sweatshirt. If something complicates it, like embroidery, it looks terrible."

Just how liberally or literally to treat the source is a question. Robert Stock claims that, "Ninety percent of the time, sportswear is a recycling process. Take, for example, most of the shirtings that we do. Their patterns come out of old textile libraries. Then we adapt certain styles of collars and pocket treatments. I'd say that everything that I do has been done before. Some styles even go back to Victorian England."

In general, since sportswear was once functional attire to be worn while playing specific sports, the original details were seldom decorative. The integrity of the designs was their utilitarianism. When sportswear is worn as everyday clothing today, some of the details are as useless as an appendix. Useless or not, we'd feel cheated if they were missing. Imagine a football jersey without the numerals. Too coy. On the other hand, imagine an exemplary specimen of a baseball jacket, kept intact, but made of satin. It's a tongue-in-cheek joke worthy of enjoyment and wearing. When active sportswear loses either its essential quality or is taken too seriously, who's trying to kid whom?

TAILORED INFLUENCE

At the opposite pole of the active sports influence is the impact of tailored clothing on casual outfittings. One variation on the tailored theme is to pluck a dress item out of its familiar context and implant it in new ground. Throwing a fine cashmere topcoat over sweat pants and a pair of combat boots is one such approach. Wearing a fatigue jacket with pleated tweed slacks is another. Juxtaposition is at the root.

The notion of juxtaposition is itself a fashion philosophy, whether one is dealing with sportswear or formalwear or the in-betweens. Juxtaposition can be carried out in large or small ways. The notion is to catch the observer unaware so he asks himself: Does he know something that I don't?

Maybe someone is wearing a navy blue suit with black wingtip shoes and brilliant red sweat socks. Wrong becomes right simply because it's being worn purposefully to challenge others' ingrained preconceptions.

Another aspect of the tailored influence is taking a piece of sportswear and treating it as a piece of tailored clothing. Back to the navy suit. Get rid of the red socks, replace them with a pair of over-the-calf ones, but take off the suit jacket. Replace it with a sweater knitted in the same style as a double-breasted blazer but in canary yellow.

What might be called the gentry look is another expression of the tailored influence. A tweedy jacket might be worn with a bulky sweater or a flannel shirt and a knit tie above baggy corduroy pants. Rather than looking like a derelict, the wearer should look like an eccentric lord tromping through the moors.

The tailored influence is part of the loosening up of menswear into an easier, more mobile mood.

LAYERED INFLUENCE

Piling on this and that and then wrapping oneself up in something else is central to the layered look. Layers become an influence on their own when the basis of the wardrobe is toppings —sweaters and/or shirts.

The idea is that traditional coats and jackets no longer exist. To make do, a fellow bundles himself with torso coverings to combat the cold, paring down as the weather becomes more temperate. Still, fearful of unpredictability, this guy always wears a sweater/shirt or two just in case.

The layered phenomenon reaches its logical apex with designers creating entire sportswear lines so that several tops combine with several other tops and vests, all of which can be worn with any number of trousers. Way back when, the approach was called mix-and-match. But then the garments were overly matched for mixing. For example, a plain shirt might have had a contrasting plaid collar that was of the same fabric as a coördinating pair of pants, while an accompanying windbreaker might have been in one color

found in the plaid and might have been lined in the exact same plaid as the shirt collar and trousers. Today, such a concoction is called "canned," a term of disparagement. Related, rather than carefully coördinated, garments epitomize the stamped-for-approval layered look. Any outfit that's too-too put-together is said to look too-too self-conscious. Colors and patterns and textures blend rather than match for optimum effect.

Of course, slender men have the physiques most suited to layering, since they can afford the additional bulk without appearing bulky. But the principles of layering can be adapted a little. The larger (but not too large) man can usually indulge in a couple of layers—say a flat-knit turtleneck sweater under a check shirt—if he steers toward receding cool colors and darker, noncontrasting patterns.

Unless one has an excellent eye for mixing pattern-on-pattern, the safer guarantee for acceptable layering is adding buffers between the patterned garments. Buffers are solid colors, often neutrals, which keep more pronounced patterns from becoming too aggressive with each other.

Since layering piles up collar treatments, guys possessing longish necks are better off capitalizing on the tactic.

GREAT OUTDOORS INFLUENCE

Layers can also be integral to a rustic mode of dressing. All the pieces share a common theme—survival in the face of austere elements—whether real or hypothetical. Storm coats, lumberjack jackets, insulated parkas, beefy overshirts, down-filled vests, pants tucked inside sweat socks, fur-lined work shoes, these are only a few of the garments falling under the spirit of the great outdoors. And hunting, fishing, mountain climbing, and shooting are only a few of the activities inspiring the outfits.

One canon of the look is that, in the usual sense of the word, the clothes don't really fit. The volume or tightness of the top contrasts greatly with the bottom, so if a flannel shirt is oversized, the khaki fatigue pants can be very snug. Or, if the carpenter pants are baggy, the corduroy shirt may contour closely to the chest. If the bottoms and tops should both be largish, that's probably so the top can carry a couple of skinny layers beneath it.

Some have said that the great outdoors influenced clothing was popularized by hunting-world sportswear operations specializing in mail order.

Others attribute the phenomenal growth to energy concerns and the wintry deep freezes of the late 70s. Still others advance the theory that the look originated in the mid-70s as a kind of reverse drag among gays. The "butch" revolution—gays expropriating the facade of ruggedness from the straight world as protest against their supposed effeminacy—is part of this questionable theory, although "butch" togs did become a conformist costume worn by many gays. As a political statement? Doubtful. That the wearers liked the sexy—to some—look is probably a better explanation. After all, straight males adopted it too.

Whoever its progenitors, clothing in the spirit of the great outdoors is a valid and significant fashion direction. It no longer carries its original sense of locale and is paraded on urban streets, bringing with it a more relaxed approach to serious clothing as well. Although the mental imagery of the great outdoorsman doesn't carry the same ramifications as the country gentleman, countrified and gentlemanly suits have picked up sturdier details, such as rifle patches and wind tabs or throat latches and reinforced elbows, all in the rugged vein. Interestingly, nearly all modern menswear is descended from English hunting clothes, so the celebration of the great outdoors returns male wearables closer to their origins.

MILITARY INFLUENCE

This is survival in another sense. A sad commentary on human history is that many items of apparel, if their ancestry isn't traced to English hunting clothes, may find their paternity in wars, far past or hauntingly recent. Fatigue pants, part of the great outdoors influence in some outfit matings, are of course more militant in their true nature. Third world politics may or may not be an issue shared by the wearers of the look, but there is something of the revolutionary or the urban guerilla about it. Of course, many of the clothes espousing the military influence cost a ransom and are shot through with designer names.

Like most extreme sportswear looks, clothing in the military style is more associated with the young. Like any fashion style, it is most effective on a well-contoured frame. The real articles, purchased at an army surplus outlet, then laundered to within an inch of their lives and only crudely pressed if at all, generally make the imitators pale by comparison. The right shoes—in this instance, boots—are all-important.

Fatigue pants with their over-sized, expandable cargo pockets cause a pear-shaped fellow to appear more bottom-heavy. Slender hips carry the style much better.

Layering is a winning strategy for adapting the military look. Navy and khaki colors plus assorted plaids are tactically correct.

The big contribution of this influence is that, by breaking apart true military uniforms and absorbing selected components into mufti, it follows that all male wearables should be nonuniform and free to adapt to new surroundings. Functional clothing assumes new connotations.

NAUTICAL INFLUENCE

Boating and yachting have always been favored themes in resortwear. Blazers, white pants and sneakers invariably look moneyed. But boating has its rougher element; that side is represented by water-repellent slickers, pea coats, bell bottom dungarees, boatnecks and the like.

Only ankle-deep in the nautical feel are breezy shorts and loose tops in bright colors or pastels that suggest sunshine more than brine.

Braids, skipper caps and status paraphernalia tend to give the look a self-conscious aspect. Clothes in the nautical vein should never look freshly purchased or landlubbery.

The classic nautical colors are navy and white, plus red. These strong contrasts are seldom smooth-sailing on stocky or rotund fellows.

SPACE INFLUENCE

Leaving the earth behind, the Space Age has less than rocketed into menswear. Futuristic designs have been launched with technical difficulties: many Earthbound fellows don't see themselves roving about à la Flash Gordon.

At its base, when it doesn't look too much like a mechanic's uniform, the one-piece jumpsuit is in the space mentality. Introduced and reintroduced every now and then with limited success, jumpsuits illustrate how space as an influence is more a passing fancy than an ongoing passion. The more successful ventures have been shiny ground crew-appearing jackets and various garments, either quilted or industrial zippered.

Until space shuttles become an everyday occurrence, space-influenced sportswear has finite possibilities. For most somatotypes, this is just as well. When the space concept is cut in sizable, shapeless garments, only the tall, slender, wide-shouldered man looks especially good in them. Read and weep, such is life.

WESTERN INFLUENCE

The West remains America's last frontier for larger-than-life heroes. The legendary cowboy lives on in sportswear.

Practicality is the key to this fashion, since the real-thing garments are the rough and tumble ones still worn by the real-people guys on the range. To them, their clothing isn't "fashion" but work clothes.

Western jeans are the basis of the look when worn on city streets. Usually worn tight, jeans don't do wonders for spreading behinds. The stereotypic image of the cowboy is tall and lean. And that's the body that fits into the style best, since the yoked-shouldered, trim lines of standard cowboy shirts are as body-conscious as the jeans. Authentic cowboy boots have pointed toes to slide more easily into the stirrups and high heels to stop the boots from slipping out. Hand-tooled leather belts with silver or turquoise buckles and leather or suede vests are also commonly part of the costume. In outerwear, shearling jackets and ranch coats are branded right.

Just how far someone goes with the Western look proves (for onlookers) whether it's a look or a fetish. The style is generally associated with the young, except in those areas of the country where cowboy gear is indigenous. There, even business suits are influenced by this ranging spirit.

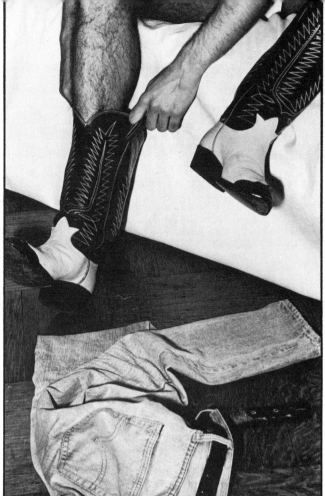

IVY INFLUENCE

The Eastern Establishment has an influence, too. It is very refined, though carried off with supposed indifference—the cashmere crewneck tied around the shoulders, the Lacoste knit shirt that sags rather than conforms to the chest, both worn with chino pants an inch too large in the waist with a perfect ribbon belt. Or with madras Bermuda shorts. Or bright corduroy pants.

The image is that the wearer comes from five generations of bankers, all of whom graduated from Harvard. In sportswear, nary an active (well, tennis and rugby pass) or a military or an outdoors or an anything-else influence invades this pristine territory of traditionalism. To appear trendy is to commit social suicide.

Depending upon how Ivy is interpreted, it is fairly easily worn without dire consequences by most body types not markedly extreme. After all, the clothing isn't supposed to make waves. But executed in golf-course colors (that's another acceptable sports influence, plus crew), this style does accentuate weight. As usual, the guy with excess girth would do better to lose it than confine his clothing choices to his waist measurement.

Although Ivy is fairly easily worn, it's not always especially flattering. Its shapelessness can appear dumpy. When the shape of the body is neither the best nor the worst, a gently shaped outfit most often creates an optical illusion for the better. "Sack" clothing is a touchy wrap-up.

REVIVAL INFLUENCE

Steeped as it is in tradition, the Ivy look could be called a revival influence. Except that the influence has never died. It simply becomes comatose from time to time.

Revivalism can be put together literally by wearing secondhand or antique clothes. The revival style can also be an updating of garments pertaining to another period but worn in a contemporary way.

Wing collar and band collar (the latter no collar really) are two shirt styles currently caught up in revivalism.

Once the only true "dress" shirt was the one gentlemen wore with formal attire. For an extended time that shirt was the wing collar shirt with its stiff, stand-up collar, corners folding back and creating the impression of wings.

During that formalized period, collars were detachable, and the starched collar was buttoned onto a neckband that circled the top of the shirt. Today's band collar shirts are much akin to the old timers minus their detachable collars.

Given the vagaries and ironies of time, by the latter 70s both wing and band collar shirts were occasionally worn under suit or sport jackets by fellows espousing liberation from conventional dressing patterns, and they had also resurfaced as sport shirts.

Whatever the particular items and however the particulars of revivalism are interpreted, this mode of dress should never appear down on its luck. Never should it look that a 50s suit jacket is being worn with denims because the guy couldn't afford a harris tweed and he happened to have discovered his father's old suit in the attic (even if he did). The outfit should look as if the wearer searched arduously for weeks in secondhand clothing stores to find that one special 50s suit jacket. Harris tweeds don't please him.

As with the tailored influence, juxtaposition is central to revivalism. If every piece of clothing is from one and the same past period, the man in the ensemble can look like a museum piece searching for a display case. Everything from different but past periods is also hard to pull off without appearing disjointed. On the whole, revivalism is more sympathetic in nonfundamentalist interpretation, when something new is added to prove the wearer isn't an amnesia victim or caught in a time warp. Faded jeans, baggy corduroy pants or khaki fatigues often do the job.

ATTITUDINAL INFLUENCE

There is no appropriate description. "Laid-back" comes close.

Although the choice of clothing may be, and probably is, painstaking, the guy projects an attitude of indifference to what he's wearing. Nothing pleases him more than appearing as if he has dressed himself in what he found that morning on the floor of his closet...except the textures, colors and patterns all come together in an offbeat way that looks fine but unpredictable.

Herculean efforts may be required to create the unlabored effect.

Layers are usually part of the attitudinal scheme. So are garments found under the other influences. Eclecticism reigns. Generally there is a sense of disproportion, or a new tangent on clothing dimensions. In classical dressing, if the clothing on the top of the body is scaled on the large size, then the proportions on the bottom are scaled down, or vice versa. In attitudinal dressing, the classical approach may be exaggerated, so that big is the biggest and small the smallest. Or,

the entire composition may be exaggerated: smocklike proportioned jackets worn with stove-pipe pants offer one alternative, while skinny-ribbed turtlenecks worn with skintight leather pants afford another.

Attitudinal dressing could also be described as rules-be-damned dressing—wearing whatever pieces appeal to you in whatever combinations. Take a classical and a *décontracté* this, a Western and an Ivy that. Combine them confidently, even belligerently, and see who salutes. Someone doesn't like the results? *Too bad.* Attitude.

From the viewpoint of the Ideal Norm, the attitudinal influence is enigmatic. Highly individ-uated, it is governed only by the wearer's, well, attitude. Although harmony should still be the praised lyrically, the music is of a different sphere. Hopefully, if the outfit's pieces are selected according to the somatotypic theory (should the attitudinal guy care to do so), this brave manner of dressing shouldn't throw his body out of whack. What the style does for him personally depends upon what he wants and from whom. But the attitudinal dresser is to be praised. He's got balls.

Chapter

6

FORMALIZING YOURSELF

Formalwear customs vary accordingly to geographic regions and—let's be honest—social strata.

BALL GAME

Etiquette be damned. Well, flouted at least.

With rules for "proper" dress dropping faster than autumn leaves in recent years, formalwear had remained the last refuge. Now the bastion has fallen.

Not that you should wear any old this-or-that to a diplomatic reception at the U.N., but clothes and Society aren't what they used to be.

On first glimpse, the rationale for dressing in formal clothing might seem weird. An executive with the American Formalwear Association says, "The most important factor in a man's decision about going formal is that he's an *escort*. If the lady on his arm is in a formal gown, then a man should be dressed accordingly, in appropriate formalwear."

Isn't this going a bit far? Are men only props?

The true rationale for formalwear is to make an occasion *special*. (Why "special" means men should dress like each other is an irrational premise we'll just have to accept as given.) Seen in an overview, the rationale for doing a formal trip makes no more nor less sense than dressing up or down for any occasion.

Vivid colors, for example, had been the rule at the English court through the Middle Ages and the Renaissance into the early 1800s, until Beau Brummell shocked sensibilities by appearing at a formal ball in startling black and white.

In the 1890s, formalwear took another upsetting turn. For decades, white tie and tails had been the thing. Bored by it all, some iconoclastic fellow commissioned his tailor to copy the traditional English smoking jacket, replete with satin lapels, for him to wear to the Tuxedo Park Ball. An immediate success it was not. But it caused a stir. Within several years, his outfit, nicknamed the tuxedo after the town in New York where it was first worn, was the reputable rule.

Now, with the rules of etiquette relaxed, color has returned. While fashion purists bemoan it, tuxedos come not only in apricot, but lemon, lime, chocolate and assorted flavors, complete with coordinated shirts and ties. When the invitation says "Black Tie," usually that enjoinder only means that the guest is expected to wear a dinner jacket or something "formal." What style or what color often is beside the point. "White Tie," though, is a more dogmatic designation, suitably answerable (etiquette still says) only in tails and, yes, white

shirt, tie and vest. But even White Tie isn't all that colorless any more. Not so long ago menswear designers became enamoured with formalwear again, but not in a flash-and-dash way. Believing that black and white are very compatible, sometimes with the introduction of a vibrant color, like red, they updated formal looks, still keeping them classic in inspiration but with some new punch. Long-absent mess jackets—short, traditionally white and terminating at the waistline—and silk robes were shown with wing collar shirts and piqué vests or cummerbunds.

One bit of trivia: cummerbunds—those broad, fitted, sashlike items that circle the waist—were initially worn as catchalls during the course of a formal dinner to keep crumbs from dropping onto a man's formal trousers. That's why the pleats face up. Considering all the etiquette involved, where were napkins?

Formalwear customs vary according to geographic regions and—let's be honest—social strata. The old guard says that a white dinner jacket is *never* appropriate in the city, even in the heat of summer. Who accepts that these days?

Formal events are either daytime or evening affairs, each time period with its own dress strictures. Six o'clock is the time barrier. Before six, daytime. After six, evening. But another qualifier is currently being used, "contemporary" or "traditional," although neither is likely to appear on an invitation. A contemporary event is less rigid, more casual, in its formalwear options. When an invitation says, "Black Tie Optional," or some such variation, such as "Black Tie or Costume," one can safely assume there's a lot of leeway. However, "optional" situations can be confusing. Events should be specified either formal or not, for when the rules of the game are clear, you decide whether or not you want to play. When invitations are vague, the only way to avoid possible embarrassment is to ask the sender to clarify. Or to steer clear.

The American Formalwear Association has been grappling with changing terminology and dicta, trying to make some sense out of what can be very confusing to most men. Here is what the organization says about a White Tie or "Full Dress" affair:

"It's a *very* special occasion. A debutant dance, a diplomatic ball or reception, a Mardi Gras ball, an important fund-raising dinner. You'll be dashing—and proper, too—in traditional full dress: a freshly starched white, wing-collared shirt, crisp white piqué vest, white tie, classic black trousers with the formal satin stripe, traditional tailcoat just covering the vest, black patent shoes."

And here's the advice for Black Tie or Black Tie Optional situations:

"You'll want to dress correctly, in a smart, comfortable tuxedo, cut almost like your newest business suit. The traditional is black, worn with white shirt and vest (or cummerbund in black or dark shades), a black tie or tie matching the cummerbund, and patent shoes."

Note the emphasis on the classics. Offbeat formalwear remains an off-the-beaten-path dressing mode, often frowned upon.

Far and away the most widely worn formal outfit is the black tuxedo. The jacket may be single- or double-breasted, with notched, peaked or shawl lapels. The lapels are usually faced with satin or sometimes grosgrain, a heavy, tightly-woven silk with horizontal ribs. A strip of satin or grosgrain runs down the outer seam of the trouser leg. Even though Amy Vanderbilt said not to, white dinner jackets often replace black ones during the summer and on cruises.

DRESS SHIRTS. Although ruffles and rainbow colors flourish, generally a subtly pleated white shirt is the standard and most acceptable one in evening formalwear. French cuffs are likewise favored. Studs—removable button substitutes, usually in gold or dark semiprecious stones—are optional.

BOW TIES. Black is the traditional color, either in satin or grosgrain. Velvet is a strong contender. Other dark colors are also worn. The choice is usually between straight bows and bigger butterfly bow ties. Designers have been pushing tiny bows in their collections, often worn in conjunction with wing-collared shirts, traditionally associated only with tailcoats.

CUMMERBUNDS. A surviving anachronism. Usually black, or coordinated (exactly or loosely) with the bow tie.

WAISTCOATS. In formalwear, this is a false-back vest, secured across the back with just a small strap. It is worn in place of, never with, a cummerbund. Black satin is standard.

SUSPENDERS. Usually worn, but for no particular reason if the trousers fit properly,

suspenders are generally black but may be other-colored for kicks. They're hardly ever visible anyway, since it ain't etiquette to remove your jacket at a fancy, formal to-do.

STOCKINGS. Note that stockings, not socks, are specified, preferably silk and black, once upon a time worn with garters.

SHOES. Black, of course. The leather should be smooth and spit-shined to perfection. Patent leather pumps—those strange low-slung slipper-appearing numbers with bows—or seamless lace-ups are preferred.

COATS. A black chesterfield coat with a velvet collar is the favored outerwear, although any dark topcoat is acceptable. A white silk scarf draped around the shoulders is an extra fillip. Some say a classic trench coat is fine in warm or wet climates, although Luciano Franzoni asserts, "Humphrey Bogart was the only man who ever looked passable with a trench coat over his tuxedo."

White tie and tails are the highly formal alternative to the basic tuxedo. Wing collars are the correct shirt style; the tie and the waistcoat are always white, usually piqué. Otherwise, the ingredients are the same.

Less formal than the classic black tuxedo are those in other colors. Tuxedos in dark brown or midnight blue are more widely approved than pastel confections.

Velvet jackets, dark business suits worn with matching or white vests, crisp shirts and smart ties contribute to the eclipse of traditional approaches to formalwear. More and more, it's the look that says formal or not. Tuxedo manufacturers get in a tizzy.

According to tradition, tails, tuxedos and white dinner jackets are never worn before six p.m. The most formal daytime outfit is comprised of the cutaway jacket—a coat cut away on a slanting line from the front, where it is fastened with a single button, to the rear, where the tails extend to just about the knees—in black or gray (this style is sometimes called a morning coat) with striped trousers, a plain vest and an ascot. "Strollers" are less formal daytime formalwear, basically gray blazerlike jackets with satin edging. Conservative suits are also appropriate in some circumstances. Only creeps hire bouncers to oust nonconforming guests.

PASSING BY

Considering the irreverent emergence of T-shirts printed to look like formalwear, it's not surprising that attitudes about tuxedos lead to far more rentals than retail sales. To rent or to buy is the quandary even for the once-a-year stepper-outer to the country club dance.

For the "different" contemporary wedding, even formalwear manufacturers will not suggest purchase. How often can a man wear a star-spangled tuxedo or be seen in a cherry pink tailcoat? On the other hand, a classic black dinner outfit is just that—a classic, even more so when single-breasted and notch-lapeled—and is acceptable year-round. If someone attends formal functions, even if only two or three times a year, buying a tuxedo makes sense, since a conservative style will surely last for several years' wear. If classic isn't someone's clothing bent, he should keep on renting.

When renting, it's always advisable to try the tux on. If possible, at least double-check every detail, including that the mandatory tailoring was indeed done. Also, are all the buttons in place? What about the accessories? Nothing is more frustrating than at the last minute discovering that something minor yet crucial is missing. Contemporary standards may be permissive, but a paperclip doesn't masquerade successfully as a pearl stud.

Even though rental prices usually include the necessary accessories (shirt, tie, studs, cummerbund or vest, but seldom shoes or outerwear without additional cost), renting the tuxedo and owning one's own accessories isn't a bad idea. An extravagance such as a satin-striped silk shirt is not that extravagant in the total scheme of things, especially if it is worn to class up or juxtapose other outfits as well. On the other hand, how often will you ever wear a silk top hat or a cane? If often, indulge. If not, good gloves (gray for daytime formalwear, white for evening), a dark chesterfield or cashmere coat (if affordable), a special bow tie or two, and your own waistcoat may be as far as you'll want to go.

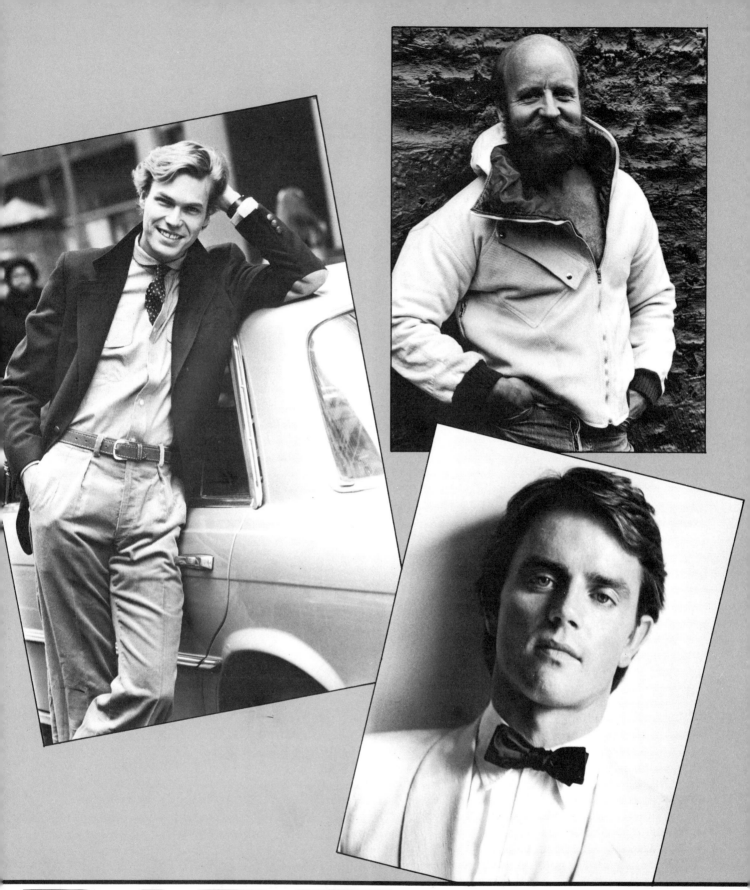

PART 3

THE WARDROBE
OUTFITTING YOURSELF

Rich as Croesus or penny-pinched, every adult male faces the same decision each morning: What to put on? Whether the selection is vast or minuscule, only a few items will be fitted on his frame daily.

At the core of every well-planned wardrobe is flexibility. Whether one chooses to look like a country squire or a country cousin, pieces of any given outfit should never be such loners that they won't participate with items from other outfits in the same or similar mood. If they can cross over the borderlines into another look entirely, that's a bonus, but not a necessity. However, the inability of clothes to adapt within a chosen style is a definite liability. Then the wardrobe appears to be comprised of a series of costumes that must be worn intact. After a while, an oft-worn outfit assumes the nature of a costume. Costumes disguise rather than illuminate the true character of the wearer. People begin to respond to the costume, not who's in it. Fine, if you want to hide behind clothing; bad, if you want to evoke spontaneous responses.

Not that you'll be mistaken for an automaton if you don't reoutfit yourself every day of the year. Who can? But a flexible wardrobe has nuances. The same necktie worn daily, but with different jackets, shirts or sweaters, can be a source of anticipatory speculation. Wearing the same tie with the same shirt and jacket once a week, year in and year out, is predictable and humdrum.

To be truly flexible, a wardrobe should allow room for surprises, though not roll-in-the-aisles guffaws. Tongue-in-cheek asides demonstrate that you're not taking yourself too seriously. On the other hand, overly lengthy wardrobes, like shaggy dog stories, can become tiresome if they drone on and on. Then it appears that you are taking clothes in general too seriously.

The distinction between too much and too little in terms of a wardrobe centers around continuity. Not wanting to look the same every day, no one should assault acquaintances with a radically altered clothing persona daily either.

Continuity, like flexibility, is a matter of degree. An entire wardrobe of whites is easier to take than an entire wardrobe of plaids. Either one certainly provides continuity, yet both are pushing it. In either instance, the wardrobe is like an autograph signed in an overly distinctive hand: the penmanship is more fascinating than the name.

Effective continuity never lets your clothes overpower you. Although the statement is hackneyed, you should wear your clothes, they shouldn't wear you.

So, a wardrobe should also be evolutionary. Indulging in an oddball purchase occasionally can add whimsy to a wardrobe and to your self-presentation. More than a few such selections, and the whole wardrobe begins to look oddball. If that's what you want, do it. Your wardrobe won't be the most workable, but it may work for you. You're never locked into any clothing choices forever.

Shuffle through some old photographs of yourself. Odds are that even though you may have loved what you were wearing *then,* the outfits look strange *now.* The clothing hasn't changed. You have. Although some styles become dated, hopefully *we* do not. But our memories play tricks on us. We often picture ourselves in the past with superimpositions of how we look, and what we wear, today.

In many ways, this trick of memory—forging the past and present into one consolidated image—and creating an evolutionary wardrobe operate on similar mechanisms. Without destroying the past, we alter it by adding bits of the present. A wardrobe is neither frozen in time—as is a particular outfit captured in a photograph—nor is it entirely of this precise moment. An evolutionary wardrobe, connecting past and present, is always moving into the future. Bridges aren't burned; they're erected. Happy crossings.

Chapter

PLANNING AHEAD

As the wardrobe grows,
so should its internal compatibility.

STORED UP

Let's get rid of a myth.

Women do *not* know how to dress men better than men know themselves. Consider the obvious. Most men are dressed by women. Most men dress badly. Ergo, what's the obvious conclusion?

In fact, a lot of women, like a lot of men, don't know how to dress themselves right. Supposedly women are much more adventurous, have a keener awareness of color and pattern, are fashion's free spirits compared to the manacled male. Myth.

Two menswear designers who also design collections for women expose the fallacy.

"Men are confused by fashion? Believe me, women are exactly the same," says Bill Blass. "That's why, when we put a collection together, we propose—we can't impose—a look. We *propose* that that's the right blouse and that's the right jacket; we propose the way a waistcoat should look, and the skirt. And women will buy that look totally. Very few will vary or experiment on their own from what the designer has shown them. Women are no more sure of their taste than men. Not at all."

"Everything in a store is sold in collections to women," points out Sal Cesarani. "The woman consumer, whom we think is the most knowledgeable about putting herself together, is already prepackaged. Even if she doesn't know it."

What makes it easier for a woman to *appear* more tasteful, adventurous and in-the-fashion-know is that generally men, unlike women, don't set out to buy total outfits. Men buy (or have women buy for them) a shirt or two here and there, some ties now and then, a suit probably only when necessary. Women, however, buy their "separates" (individual garments) at the same time to relate one with the other. The odds of achieving consistently good results are automatically improved. Besides, the simple truth is that most women spend more time and money on dressing right. It's harder for them to fail. But fail they can and do, just like men. Successful dressing, for either gender, requires some digging in and striking out on one's own, and enthusiasm.

"If a man is married and his wife brings him his ties home," notes Ralph Lauren, "he's going to be befuddled in the morning about what goes with what. But if he buys his own clothes, he can put

himself together."

Of course, the reverse is also true. If a woman doesn't involve herself in her wardrobe selection and abdicates her decisions to someone else, she'll be befuddled too.

An odd assortment of clothing can't be called a wardrobe. Plotting a wardrobe without premeditation is criminal.

NO-FAULT INSURANCE

In wardrobe planning, one's somatotype is inconsequential. What matters is laying out sound strategy. Presumably the tactics will be the same for everyone. Or will they?

Ralph Lauren remarks, "A man who doesn't really know how to put himself together should make sure that his wardrobe is as uncomplicated as possible, leaving little room for error. Classic, simple stripes; basic colors; basic colored shirts. Nothing very complicated. Everything very, very simple. You can never go wrong with that. And, in most cases, it's a better look. Less is more. If a man wears simpler clothes that fit well, that's all he's got to do."

Unquestionably, Lauren's statement is the most commonly heard advice within the menswear industry. Stick to the classics, the theory goes, and you're in like flint. Ask the experts to propose a basic male wardrobe, and the nominees invariably consist pretty much of the following.

GRAY FLANNEL VESTED SUIT. Preferably single-breasted, with notched lapels. Trousers can be worn with other suit and sport jackets. The vest is another spare part.

NAVY BLUE VESTED SUIT. Single-breasted preferred, but double-breasted acceptable. In a blazer-suit style, so the jacket can act as a blazer, the trousers as sport slacks and the vest as another mixable.

CHECK SPORT JACKET. Single-breasted only. Non-seasonal weight. Subtly scaled, the pattern should be non-emphatic for greater flexibility.

DRESS SHIRTS. Emphasis on solid colors, particularly white and light blue, with a couple of pin stripes.

TIES. Neat, foulard patterns, diagonal stripes, solids.

SLACKS. Camel flannel. Tan corduroy. Jeans.

147

No one can deny that such a wardrobe is a Sure Thing. But it may not be a Fun Thing.

Chip Tolbert says, "A gray flannel suit is not necessarily unexciting. You start with the very basic things that you can wear over and over again without somebody saying, 'Oh, Jesus, is he wearing that suit again?' American men are very lax about accessorizing, putting together an outfit once they have the components.

"The biggest single mistake is to buy six shirts at one time because you simply need shirts," the fashion director continues, "rather than adding to your wardrobe each season. If you buy a wardrobe all at once, you miss out on new things as they come out. Every man should try to develop his own style. Just because something is shown in a fashion magazine, that doesn't mean the look is right for him. But there are always versions or adaptations that are right. One only has to look around for them. A lot of men are lazy. Looking at other men to see how they're dressed, being aware, is a habit many men haven't formed."

Building a basic wardrobe is the logical first step in wardrobe planning. The *first,* not the *final* step. But "basic" needn't be the gray flannel syndrome. If your life doesn't revolve around

wearing suits in the classic manner, decide what your own classics are. They may all be casual items—jeans, corduroy baggies, an assortment of sweaters. Still, the principle is the same: as the wardrobe grows, so should its internal compatibility. (Compatibility stems from the proper blending of texture, color and pattern, plus stylistic continuity if desired.) Clothing purchases are investments toward long-term togetherness.

How long can you reasonably expect the relationship to last? Truthfully, you can never know for certain. Longevity or its lack depends upon how trendy any garment is, whether the trend becomes full-grown fashion or fizzles, at what point in the fashion cycle an item is purchased, et cetera, et cetera. If you've the money, you can afford to gamble. If not, maybe you'd prefer gambling anyway.

"For me, 'investment clothes' are clothes that can be worn for two or three years," says Bill Kaiserman. "If we're dealing in fashion, we're dealing in fashion. Fashion is a changing thing.

"What I design every year is, to me, not trendy," he continues. "It's what I believe *at the moment* is the *permanent* fashion. When you're a designer, you can't be skeptical, you have to have one-

hundred-percent-pure belief. But I find that when I look at some of my designs from four or five years ago—things I thought were absolutely classic—the proportions are always slightly off at this particular moment.

"To make something that is only good for this year is much too extreme. My mind seems to work in a three-year cycle. But I'll make a blue blazer till I stop designing. And gray flannel pants.

"The shaping and the proportions of the blazer or those pants make the fashion," Kaiserman asserts. "To me, fashion is much more governed and changed by shapes, not fabrics. A beautiful fabric is a beautiful fabric and always will be. It's the silhouette that changes fashion.

"A look never comes back in exactly the same way. If it did, there'd be no need for designers. We could just have recycle people doing clothes.

"A wardrobe doesn't stay the same. You and your wardrobe are in a state of constant change. There's something fantastic about updating your suit while at the same time wearing an old shirt. And then updating the shirt when perhaps you're wearing a four-inch tie. And then changing the suit and coming in with a skinny tie.

"It's evolution," Kaiserman goes on. "There's something very exciting about part of what you're wearing being severe fashion and the other part being obviously not. Otherwise, you become a fashion plate. In the negative sense. When you're forever throwing everything out and getting everything new at the same time, you become *boom*. There's something very false about that.

"In the end result, a person should be able to go to his closet, find things that he loves, and put them on. There's no logic in discarding everything at one shot and coming in with everything new at another shot. No one—not even a clothes designer—can be that erratic in his loves," Kaiserman concludes.

HIGH RANKING

Just as a single article of clothing has no real meaning until it's worn as part of an outfit, your wardrobe is not an abstraction either. Clothes—and wardrobes—are to be worn enjoyably. To get the most from them, you have to know your way around.

How simple or complicated your wardrobe needs to be depends upon how complex your lifestyle is or isn't. Suppose you work in a place where casual clothing is acceptable; assume you never go to restaurants where suits and ties are expected; you attend rock, not symphonic, concerts; you're an at-homer, not an on-the-towner. If this rather consistent routine describes your life, you may not own a suit and presumably don't need one. Your wardrobe can revolve around casual pants, shirts and sweaters. As long as the textures, colors and patterns are compatible, you're all set.

On the other hand, if your activities are varied, you place greater demands on your wardrobe. If your job requires suits or sport jackets, you automatically have more clothing concerns to cope with. Away from the business milieu, you may sometimes appear in dress clothes, but more likely you'll want less uptight outfits for at-home entertaining or relaxed weekending. If you're a theater buff, you might want some dressier clothes or accessories than you normally wear during the day. If you go roller discoing, you'll want to wear something else again.

A workable wardrobe includes all the necessary pieces to see you through the day, the night, the weekend and special occasions without it appearing that you've messed up your appointment book. Presumably, the more you do, the more different types of clothes you need. *Unless* you invest in adaptable clothes that can fulfill the requirements for several situations.

First, though, you must determine your clothing expectations, not just your needs. The best way is to get paper and pencil and start making lists. Divide the page vertically into four columns. In the first column, record all the activities you'll probably pursue during the next few weeks. Be specific. Don't simply write down "leisure activities." Designate them precisely, such as neighborhood movies, Saturday night poker, et cetera.

After compiling these functions, think about any event or occasion that might be coming up. Be hypothetical. You might write down a possible job interview, a wedding or a funeral, a vacation in Acapulco, if any of these seem remotely possible.

In the next column, enter a brief description of the type of clothing you feel you should, or would like to, wear on these occasions. This time, don't be too specific. Don't put in actual outfits. Rather, pinpoint "suits," "jeans and sweater," "hot outfit," "sport jacket and casual pants," et cetera.

Now the list gets a little harder to complete. In the third column, estimate the approximate percentage of your time you will spend following all the pursuits over a certain period, say a month.

Finally, in the last column, make a subjective analysis of how significant the activities are *to you* in terms of how you look. A little soul-searching, please. Are you more concerned about your appearance on the prowl than on the job, at the Saturday brunch or your mother's Sunday dinner?

This compilation should help you view your wardrobe in three ways. (1) By outlining your usual activities, you can see at once what type of clothing corresponds to most of your undertakings. Logically, if you wear casual clothing for more activities than suits, then sportswear should make up the bulk of your basic wardrobe. *However,* (2) if you spend a greater percentage of your time in dress clothes, maybe suits should be given greater importance in your wardrobe even if most of your activities numerically are casual. *But,* (3) what about your own values? Maybe one of the recorded events—perhaps the job interview or the disco—doesn't occur all that often. Still, if you've given it a four-star rating, then clothes for that occasion might demand your best attention and your greatest wardrobe effort.

No one can establish your priorities for you. But priorities must be set before your wardrobe can really get going. Obviously you require clothing for all the activities listed. After determining what outfits are truly the most important in your lifestyle, then you should rank other garments in descending importance. If a sport jacket is lowest on the list, perhaps you'll want to forget about owning one entirely and replace it with a handsome cardigan sweater that can also be worn with a shirt and tie.

The surest way to keep the wardrobe running smoothly is to possess major items in harmonious colors, textures and patterns, so they can shift gears and make new connections. Without flexible items and outfits, the mechanisms of the wardrobe break down.

If finances are problematical, stick to non-seasonal fabrics. Nubby tweeds look terrific and can be terrifically hot during sultry summers. A trench coat with a zip-out lining will get you through more days and evenings throughout the year than a summer-weight gabardine topcoat.

It's always smarter to think in terms of outfits rather than isolated pieces, although outfits can be planned around single garments. Take a pair of chocolate brown corduroy pants. Add a rust plaid flannel shirt and a suede vest, that's one outfit. With the same pants, a tan button-down shirt, an orange Shetland crewneck and a tan poplin

blouson jacket make up another look for another occasion. But any of the pieces can form the basis of other outfits. The crewneck can be worn with the plaid shirt and gray twill pants. The suede vest can be worn with the gray pants, the tan button-down shirt, a tie and a seasonless blazer. On and on the wardrobe shifts, outfit by outfit, occasion into occasion.

DOUBLE VISION

To judge the success or failure of your present wardrobe, you've got to know the items in it.

The following routine may presuppose more clothing than you actually own. If so, substitute the outfits you normally wear for the dressiest occasions you engage in for the specified suits. What you're investigating is a method of becoming more familiar with your present wardrobe's actual potential. Unfortunately, if you can't improvise this number, face the fact that your wardrobe's flexibility is seriously limited by your limited amount of clothing.

Lay out three suits side by side. Say you have a gray flannel suit (everybody says you should), a brown glen plaid suit and a navy pin striped one. Combine and recombine them, trying the jacket of one with the pants of the others. If any suits are vested, try out the vests too, sometimes matching the jacket, other times the pants, alternately matching neither.

By now you should be seeing your suits as they really are, potentially odd pieces that can split and go their separate ways.

Now bring out more suits if you have them, or sport jackets, additional pants and vests. Add them to the three suits and organize them into three stacks: one of your jackets, another of your pants, and the last of vests. Separate each of the three piles into color families, all the grays together, the browns together, et cetera.

Now bring out six or eight shirts, plus four or five sweaters. Arrange these together in color families also. First combine the shirts and sweaters with jackets in the same color family, say blue with blue. Then see what happens mixing color families, say blues with browns. Keep mental—or actual—notes of combinations you particularly like. After running through the jackets, move on to the stack of pants. Again, keep mental or actual notes about pleasing combinations.

Don't allow your mind to become boggled—if it

isn't already. This time, try to make appealing trios out of appealing duos, placing the shirt in the central position. That is, see what happens when both the jacket and the pants you like with the same shirt come together in concert. Repeat this exercise with several shirts and the jackets and pants you liked with them separately.

If most of the trios are at odds with each other, either your wardrobe is exorbitantly large or exceedingly mismanaged.

You can, and should, experiment with casual clothing, following the same routine to discover if pleasing twosomes yield satisfactory threesomes, and under what circumstances.

By shifting and rearranging all your clothing, it should soon become apparent if your wardrobe is overburdened with strong patterns but light on more easily mixable solids, or if its colors leap all over the lot without harmonizing or complementing each other enough of the time.

While you've been examining the pieces, perhaps you've discovered some garments you haven't worn in ages. If you haven't worn them, why not? Because you don't like them? Call the Salvation Army. Because they don't fit? Get them, or yourself, in shape; either they or you can possibly be flatteringly altered. Unworn clothes are dead weights and confuse the issue.

You've done enough for one day. Almost. Return your clothes to their proper places. Go out and buy a full-length mirror. Tomorrow you'll test your memory and your eyes. At random, you'll pull out a suit or sport jacket, and you'll actually try it on with a couple of shirt-and-trouser combinations you thought looked good with it. And you'll try out several ties and vests or sweaters to see how they fit into the totality. Give yourself a solid two hours or more.

While it's a bore at first, trying on different combinations will build your confidence, so later you can make your choices inside your head. Even then, the full-length mirror will confirm or deny your mental evaluations.

(P.S. You have no plans to try the above experiments, do you? Your loss. How the hell do you expect to get your act together without any rehearsal? Think about it.)

COLOR KEYED

If your wardrobe isn't making it, one of the easier ways to help shape it up is to confine all new purchases to one color family, with little or no patterns to the garments. Doing so should impose some immediate discipline over your unruly clothing collection. During your next outing, buy only items in another color family but one harmonious with the pieces you bought on the first go-round. Since solids are automatically more versatile, you should now have more mixable options.

Over a period of time, add new colors and patterns as you will and can. Allowing for prudent discards, your wardrobe will not grow appreciably in size, but the clothes you now own should stretch much further.

Making suggestions about what specific items to purchase, and when, is impossible. There are too many variables, the most important of which is your desire. But don't try to move too fast. Shooting your wad in one load is premature.

Dressing right isn't a slam-bam, you're-through affair. Your reasons for wanting to master your wardrobe shouldn't be confined to alleviating clothing worries. Once the headaches are gone, dressing right is no longer a pain. It's a positive pleasure. Like anything good, keep it going. Dressing right is somewhat like sex. Once you've got the techniques down pat, that surely isn't the time to stop. With experience, the real fun begins.

SUM TOTAL

You've heard it before and you'll hear it again: *Keep your eyes open.*

Because of social conditioning, most men don't really look at other men, possibly because they're afraid of being caught in the act. Get over it. Women constantly watch other women, learning a lot in the process. By seeing what works and what doesn't in other men's wardrobes, you'll have a much clearer conception of your opportunities.

Look around you. Look at men on the street, the models in men's fashion magazines, the photographs in this book. You won't want to emulate every male you see; you'd become schizophrenic.

And while it's smart to study fellows of your own general size and age whom you consider well-dressed, sizing up only those fellows is too narrow a focus. You're limiting your possibilities. Some stranger half or twice your age or size could help you discover a new way to tie your muffler.

Be on the lookout for techniques you'd never think of trying without first seeing how they work, such as wearing Indian-beaded moccasins with levis and a classic blazer with a hooded sweatshirt beneath it. If it looks good on him, who's to say it won't look better on you? *Remove your blinders.* You're slotting yourself, and others are ready to do that for you.

Know something? By learning to express yourself freely, you free yourself. And the air breathes clean.

Chapter

8

ADDING ON

Accessories flesh out a sturdy wardrobe's skeleton.

DRESS REHEARSAL

No small parts? Only small players?

If the major participants of your wardrobe are working well, minor issues like accessories do gain in stature. But if the big things don't make it, little things remain little things, much ado about next-to-nothing. Realistically, no supporting actor ever saved a rotten show. A mediocre show, possibly. But only when the production is tip-top can supporting roles really shine.

The skeleton of a wardrobe is its major pieces, those that carry the heaviest load and are worn most often. In general, these garments are on the conservative, understated side to act as backdrop. Accessories can't turn a flop into a triumph, but they can class up an already good act. Accessories flesh out a sturdy wardrobe's skeleton. They can transform a basically plain outfit into a handsome one, and they can change an essentially strong outfit into a high-voltage *tour de force*.

MAKING HEADWAY

Male headgear has been steadily inching back in popularity since the big plummet during the long-haired days of doing your own thing.

The difference between caps and hats is that a hat has a brim completely surrounding the crown, but a cap has only a partial or no brim. Thus, some fabric "caps," in truth, are hats because their brims are continuous.

Coty Award-winning hat maker, Marsha Akins, who heads up Makins Hats, says, "Men who haven't gotten into hats have a lot of misconceptions about them. Does wearing a hat make you bald faster? Absolutely not. Will hats leave marks on the forehead or mat the hair? Only if they're too heavy or don't fit correctly. Hats should rest on the head, not squeeze it. Will hats make you perspire more? Leather sweatbands might, not those made of ribbon. But if a hat is too tight, you'll perspire more. Do hats require reblocking and special care? Not if they're treated with the common courtesy of resting them flat on a shelf. Must a man remove his hat in a restaurant? I don't think so. If it's proper for a woman to keep on her hat, why shouldn't it be for a man? It's that old division-of-sex-roles bullshit."

Conventional practice argues against her view of hat etiquette.

Hats are no longer considered a social necessity and have become a staid or flippant option, depending upon how they are worn.

The usual business or dress hat comes in a snap-

brim style. Most often of plain felt with a silk or ribbon band, it is worn with the brim turned down in front, snapped up in back. Generally the crown has a center crease or two indentations at both sides in the front. Some shorter brimmed styles with lower crowns are worn all turned down and creaseless.

Many snap-brim hats—especially the bucket-shaped, narrow-brimmed Irish cloth numbers in various tweeds, and the Tyrolean hat, similar to the style donned by Swiss yodelers—are not considered dress hats but are worn with suits and topcoats regardless.

But it is in sportswear that hats and caps do most of their flinging. They give a new angle to the casual attitude. Rather than injecting a note of sobriety, most raise a little hell.

HEAVY NECKING

Ties don't have to be a serious business.

One offshoot of traditional neckties might be called the have-knot direction. A purposeful sense of disarray or forgetfulness accompanies the have-knot appearance. A conventional knot may be slipped to one side or the upward journey to the shirt collar isn't completed. The tie may be tied in a quick flip, producing only a single loop, and is then left stranded, as if memory failed. Or the tie may be passed under the unbuttoned shirt collar with nary a loop or a knot at all, disqualifying it from being a true have-knot, but producing the same impression of supposedly chic dishevelment or senility. The have-knots are a tangent of attitude dressing.

Neckwear that is commonly referred to as an ascot might more properly be called a cravat. The true ascot, sometimes seen at formal daytime weddings, has wide, usually squared ends that are worn, after the neck has been looped twice, folded diagonally one over the other and held in place by a jeweled or plain stickpin. The name is derived from Ascot Heath, where cutaway-clad Englishmen often appear in ascots to view the races.

A neckcloth that's tied or folded in front and tucked into the top garment is called a cravat, from the French *cravate*. The word is occasionally used interchangably with necktie. Croatian mercenaries of the French government introduced linen neckscarves in that country during the 17th century. The style was first adopted by women, by

men later, and finally crossed the Channel to England, dropping the final *e* en route.

Cravats can be folded in many, sometimes intricate, ways, but the most widely-worn method is in the so-called ascot manner—looped once with a single knot under the chin and usually draped into a shirt or sweater.

Considering how vague the menswear vocabulary is, it's amazing that anyone ever learns how to dress.

Cravats are also sometimes called scarves. This might be because in the early 1900s the term necktie and scarf were synonymous, which offers no help to today's menswear vocabulary.

Essentially, a scarf is a piece of fabric wider than a conventional necktie and in varying lengths, worn draped around the shoulders or tied in one way or another around the neck. Twisted handkerchieves would be scarves in a necking routine.

Mufflers are longer-dimensioned, perhaps narrower, versions of scarves. Once worn for warmth, today many are decorative as well and may be sported indoors with a flipped-up jacket collar. Mufflers can be knitted or woven, whereas many scarves are woven fabrics of cotton, wool, silk or other natural fibers or of fiber blends.

How scarves and mufflers are worn can be individualistic, even idiosyncratic. In attitude dressing, it's not unusual to wear two or more, sometimes twisted together, sometimes not. Longer versions may be tied at the ends but not around the throat. Or other ways too. If the unusual is done with flair, it's right.

PEEKING OUT

Pocket squares have no practical purpose. They're tucked inside breast pockets for show, a flash of color or a dash of pattern. Usually made of silk or fine fabrics, they aren't designed for nose-blowing or forehead-wiping.

There is no "correct" way to fold a pocket square. Points can extend in a triangle or in a flower petal motif, or the square can be shoved in and puffed however you choose, points up or hidden.

White linen is often worn for dressier events, but not exclusively.

WRAP AROUNDS

Properly fitted pants aren't about to fall off, but belts still make their wardrobe rounds.

With suits, belts usually try to be inconspicuous. In fact, with vests, belts shouldn't be worn at all, since they cause the midsection to lump. When seen, belts are usually in the same general color as the shoes—brown with brown, black with black.

Sport belts are another dimension. Sometimes they're not belts at all, but merely lengths of hemp, rawhide or rope, wrapped around and knotted. Fabric and even neckties can perform this trick. So-called ribbon belts may be worn tied or looped or otherwise fastened for effect rather than efficiency. Buckles may get a big play.

Belts can add a great deal of interest, sometimes too much. If body proportions aren't the best, oversized or even small but brightly colored belts can cut the physique in half, drawing attention to any deviations from the Ideal Norm. Wide white belts on wide paunches are glaring examples of belts leading the wearer astray.

Some pants have self-belts or extension waistbands which are more trimming than belted

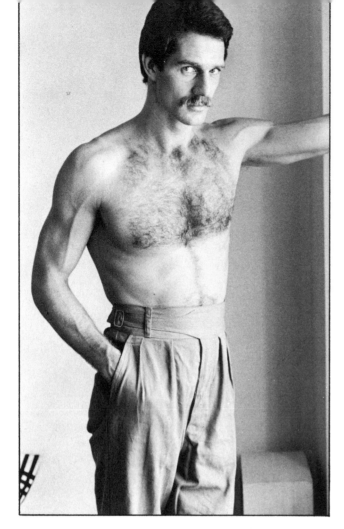

trousers for larger bodies, but these look best on fellows with slim waists and broad shoulders.

FOOT NOTES

Since dressing right is a head-to-toe business, shoes and socks have their input too.

Most importantly, shoes must fit perfectly. While heavier shoes make big feet appear bigger and wingtips are too decorative for rotund bodies, you should worry less about shoe styles hurting an outfit than the shoes literally hurting you. If narrow shoes are popular and your feet are like a duck's, don't try to squeeze into the times.

Although shoes are available in all colors and styles, dress shoes generally come in black, brown or cordovan leather. (Suede shoes, even in dressed-up cap toes, are still considered on the casual side.) Usually black shoes are worn with blues and black; brown shoes with other browns; cordovans with browns and some blues. Gray clothing may be paired with any of the three leather colors. Smooth leathers are thought of as dressier than grained ones.

Lighter leathers, two-tone combinations such as spectator or saddle shoes, canvas and cloth shoes, bucks and sneakers stride about more sportily. Boots are seldom if ever dressy.

Several theories suggest how shoes and socks should relate. One notion says that if the shoes are dark, the socks should be dark too, in similar or harmonious colors, so that knobby ankles aren't too outstanding. The rationale for another theory suggests that socks and trousers should be in similar colors and values, also to downplay ankles. Yet another notion is that shoes should fairly much correspond to the lightness or darkness of the pants, with the shoes always being somewhat darker and the socks matching either—tan shoes with beige pants, tan or beige socks; beige shoes with white pants, beige or white socks. The most absolutist concept is that socks should pick up some color, texture or pattern from the shirt or tie.

As usual, the shoe and sock theories are more adamantly advanced for dress outfits. A man's dress hosiery is always to reach at least to mid-calf, preferably over the calf, since seeing a male shin, horror of horrors, is supposed to be gauche. Most socks worn with suits are pretty subdued. Ribbon stitches (alternating raised and lowered

ribs running vertically) and clock stitching (small design motifs along the side of the sock) fairly well cover the conventional approach to toeing the line with business attire. Checks and argyles are relatively sporty. Crew socks are true sportswear.

Common sense is a truer guide than elaborate philosophies. Having a wardrobe of shoes is highly recommended, but affordability factors creep in. The wrong shoes definitely can make an outfit appear askew. Simple loafers and oxfords are more adaptable than jogging shoes or formal pumps. Socks in gray, brown and black are more mixable than green argyles. But safety isn't always praiseworthy.

In short, shoes and socks deserve as much attention as shirts and pants. They are finishing touches, but touches nonetheless. Little things do mean a lot.

IN BRIEF

Undershirts, skivvies, pajamas and the like are usually not for public viewing. Here you can indulge any fantasies or forget the matter entirely. Chances are anyone with whom you're intimate enough to expose the private inner workings of your wardrobe doesn't have tasteful color coordination uppermost in mind.

Then again, there's more to all clothing than public viewing. How any garments, even the unseen ones you're wearing, make you *feel* is way up there in importance. It's ironic that bikini underwear has exploded in popularity, while many men are otherwise still conservative with their exterior clothing expressions. Why has underwear taken on flamboyant shades? Probably because getting off on one's briefs is purely and simply a happy thing to do. All clothing should have some of that charge. Could it be, as these hidden flourishes suggest, that lots of guys have creative or crazy or nonconformist impulses they'd like to release just for the hell of it? Underneath it all, the evidence appears strong. Come out of the shell. Swagger a little.

PRACTICE

THE BIG STEP

ASSERTING YOURSELF

SHOPPING AROUND

STEPPING OUT

So you want to dress right. And you know you can. Only one stumbling block stands in your way. Shopping.

A lot of men get sweaty palms entering a men's clothing store or department, and with some good reason. Often, if the sales staff isn't lurking in the shadows, ready to pounce, the clerks are so self-occupied that one can feel like an intruder. Or the salesmen are so nattily dressed themselves, you feel you have no chance of looking even half that good.

Before beginning a clothes hunt, you've got to prime yourself, thickening your skin for the process. If you merely want to browse and a clerk is hovering about, simply say, "I'd prefer looking on my own. When I need some help, I'll let you know." Conversely, if you want to be shown something in particular and the salesperson is a butterfly, net him with, "Excuse me, but I only have a few minutes. Would you help me please?"

An arrogant attitude will not ingratiate you with sales people, but being firmly insistent should get results. If not, you're in the wrong store. You're there to be served, not intimidated, nor ignored.

"Men should get over insecurities about shopping," says Sal Cesarani, who emerged from a retail background himself. "After all, your dollars are buying not only a product that's hopefully reputable and has endurance, but you're buying service and what the store represents."

One psychological ploy is to shop with a woman or a very turned-out male friend. (Let your companion know in advance if you want her or his assistance in choosing or in decoying.) Sales people are so stuck on the notion that most men can't shop for themselves that they will focus their attention and sales spiels on your cohort. You can half-listen or tune out, going about your business unmolested. But don't be totally deaf. Often the store's personnel will have very sound suggestions about clothing coordination. Certainly they know the stock better than you do. Taking advantage of their expertise is only smart.

When you find several garments that you like, try all of them on. But control any impulses to buy. Now. Deciding to allocate a whole day (or several days) to looking, before purchasing, will expose you to more options. Even if you have to retrace your steps, this is the better way to greater decisiveness about what you truly want.

Recognize that many stores and/or men's departments have their own image to project, as a trendsetter, a tower of conservatism, whatever.

"Men have a habit of going to one store only.

172

Their choice is automatically limited to what that store offers," notes Chip Tolbert. "One of the major faults with American men is that they're too damned lazy to shop around."

Shop around so you're not locked into one store's fashion image. As you check out different stores, you should try on various outfits. If sales people consider you a royal pain, fine.

Naturally, there's more to clothing—and shopping—than personal style. Knowledge of the relative relationship between quality and price; the importance of proper fit; the care required for maintaining clothing; all fall within shopping wisely and asserting yourself.

MONEY CLIP

Only the little boy at the processional was indiscreet enough to point out that the pompous emperor knew absolutely nothing about his new clothes, although his royal posterior made the fact perfectly clear. In fact, why one suit is superior to another remains pretty much invisible to an untrained eye.

"Quality is particularly hard to pinpoint in men's clothing where so much of the fine craftsmanship is hidden," says Walter B.D. Hickey, Jr., president of Hickey-Freeman, the suit maker known for its quality and price tags. "A suit must be painstakingly balanced, yet a customer is only interested in his appearance and comfort after purchasing it."

"For that price, it's got to be good," is the sentiment too often voiced by men who equate price with quality. Maybe yes, maybe no.

Designer suits almost always cost more than those without designer labels. This higher price may reflect fabric choices and workmanship, or the fact that many designers collect royalties for the use of their names on the label. Otherwise, the price of a man's suit has little to do with so-called fashion. Principally, the quality of the fabric and the amount of labor involved in producing the garment determine its cost.

Hand-tailoring is obviously more expensive than machine-run operations. But then there's style. *Apparent* value is more important for most men than *intrinsic* value.

Value also relates to one's wallet.

"Building a wardrobe depends upon a man's income," Chip Tolbert points out. "If someone has limited income and it's possible for his wardrobe to cross over into various phases of his life, so much the better. Then he seemingly has a larger wardrobe. But it's terribly easy to be ripped off. It is quite possible to get a very good suit for $150 or $200. You just have to look harder. The less money one has, the more one should shop around. Only by shopping more do you find value. It's also the only way that you learn quality."

Quality fabrics often have the *feel* of quality. Step inside a fabric shop. Locate two different grades of wool at markedly different prices. Squeeze both of them in your hand. The more costly one will feel softer and richer. Find some cashmere fabric. It will be softer and richer still. However, don't be misled. The cashmere may not have greater "value" just because it costs more. Unlined cashmere pants would sag at the knees and hold no shape. A cheaper wool might be the better choice, especially when the clothing budget is tight.

Affordability factors aside, certain guidelines exist to help in determining if a suit is well-made.

• Check out the seams. Any puckers indicate poor workmanship.

• Investigate the stitching. Hand-sewing is a mark of quality, particularly at the collar and on the lapels. Stitches by hand are always a bit more irregular than those by machine.

• Look for a jacket collar contoured to cling to the neck. There should be no buckled space between shirt and jacket collars. A softer "roll"— the softness of the turning fabric—to the collar should rest more naturally than a stiff one.

• The lapel points should be well-defined. Give the lapels a squeeze to test if they resume their original shape. If properly made, they will without wrinkling.

• The shoulder line should be smooth and well-formed from the neck to the sleevehead (the top of the sleeve where it attaches to the armhole).

• The sleeveheads, purposefully larger than the armholes for freedom of movement and shoulder padding, should be precisely sewn (preferably by hand) to distribute fullness without wrinkles or puckers. Armholes should have sweat shields.

• On finer suits, buttonholes are hand-sewn, and the buttons are not sewn too closely to the fabric. A "neck" of thread from fabric to button makes fastening more managable.

• Check pattern matching. If the suit is striped, for example, the pattern should match at the seams from sleeve to torso, from pocket to jacket, at the lapels and throughout the suit.

- Vents should be properly aligned. If either side is dragging lower than the other, the jacket's proportions will be askew.
- The lining of the jacket should be smooth. Inferior interiors suggest inferior quality, despite outward appearances. However, whereas many European-made suits are fully lined, most expensive American-made ones have only half or three-quarter linings. In more contemporary styles, there is a shift away from lining entirely.
- Check the seams and workmanship of trousers as well.
- Rub the waistband between your thumb and forefinger. You should feel some interior reinforcement, otherwise the band may roll when worn.

Although these aspects can be checked by eye, other elements of construction—such as the amount of pressing during early stages to iron "memory" into seams—are not readily apparent.

Prices of suits go up proportionately with the number of steps to produce them. More steps by hand add dollars to the price tag. Whatever a suit's price, if the cost of alterations is not included, a man must be prepared to pay more to ensure proper fit. An inexpensive suit well-contoured to the wearer's body is worth more than a quality suit three sizes too big.

Also related to value is need, pure and simple. If you require a suit for business, a sturdy business suit is more valuable to you than an all-silk tropical suit. Before shopping for a suit, you should predetermine your reasons for buying and, as much as humanly possible, exactly what you want. A black sharkskin dinner suit at half price is no bargain if your goal was to replace an out-of-style gray flannel.

From a strictly utilitarian point of view, a conservative suit has greater longevity within a wardrobe, hence it has more value over an extended period of time in that it probably will not need to be replaced as often as a more look-at-me style. For this reason, men are most often advised to invest their major bucks in basics and classics instead of passing clothing fancies. Doing so is perfectly logical and can be perfectly dull, *unless* the basics and classics are genuinely handsome and desirable. A smart gray flannel suit looks better than a dumb one. Even so, allocations for

spirit-injecting accessories—shirts, ties, sweaters, belts, pocket squares—shouldn't be ignored.

And let's not forget the psychological value of dressing right. When you know that you look good, odds are you're going to feel fine, and what's better than that? If an outfit picked up in a thrift shop picks you up, it's worth more, to you, than the finest suit you can't stand. True clothing value, high- or low-priced, makes you feel like dancing.

FITTING IN

Superior quality is worthless if a garment doesn't fit. If clothes are to make the most of your body, they've got to be intimately involved with it.

Not surprisingly, even concerning fit, sportswear is in a class all its own. Usually proper fit is described as being neither too loose nor too tight: apparel should encase the body comfortably without stretching or buckling.

Terrific, except sportswear garments are often worn purposefully tight or baggy either to accentuate the shape of the clothes or to emphasize body-consciousness.

Only in tailored clothing are there reasonably standardized guidelines for proper fit. But *décontracté* suits are most often purposefully worn with a sportswear attitude, with the proportions sometimes larger, the fit often looser. Ivy League jackets are usually worn shorter than British ones, and British hacking jackets are longer still than other British models. A long Ivy jacket and a short hacking jacket are both "improper."

What's a good fit could also be viewed as what's flattering for particular physiques. A longer jacket length on a short man further abbreviates his stature. Paradoxically, longer jackets lengthen tall men too. Even when jacket lengths are fashionably longer, the "right" longer ones are improper for both short and tall men when evaluated in terms of the Ideal Norm.

To further complicate matters, conventional suit jackets should *always* extend to cover the buttocks (according to the time-accepted rule), so any jackets that don't are "improper" at the outset, fashion or the Ideal Norm notwithstanding.

Once again, we're forced to view a subject with relative judgment and with an awareness that the clothing scene changes.

Generally, though, we are inclined to commit the same mistakes over and over, regardless of changing fashion silhouettes or trends.

"American men have always been concerned first and foremost with comfort. That's why most wear their clothes two sizes too big—armholes down to their waists, jackets four inches too full, pants baggy," remarks Chip Tolbert. "Men go into stores and do calisthenics when trying on a suit. Well, they don't do calisthenics when they wear their suits, so it's idiotic. A suit you can do jumping jacks in has to look sloppy in repose."

Although proportions will change somewhat according to fashion, the overall signs of a properly fitting suit remain fairly consistent.

A jacket should drape smoothly over the torso, front and back, with no wrinkles and no signs of stress. There should be no gap between the jacket collar and the shirt collar. Similarly, the body of the jacket should rest securely on the torso without any buckling between the lapels and the collar bones. Jacket sleeves should stop about five inches above the tip of the thumb and should allow a flash of shirt cuffs to extend out from under them, about a quarter of an inch or so. Jacket lengths, though variable, can be tested by letting your arms hang straight by your sides, then curling your hands as if to make half-fists. The bottom edge of the jacket should rest comfortably within the curvature of your hands.

Trousers should rest firmly and comfortably around the waist and hips without pulling or drooping. Any wrinkling exposes a poor fit. Pants in the proper length, another variable, barely touch the top of the shoe but are long enough to form a slight "break" in the trousers.

Naturally, proper fit is a bit more complicated than the foregoing suggests. The garments worn beneath the suit, weight fluctuations, posture, all these and more affect a suit's fit. But nothing is more crucial than the alterations when purchasing a new suit.

To insure proper fit, you must start off on the right foot, meaning you have to do some preplanning and some predressing for the occasion.

First, you should have a general idea of the type of suit you want: its basic style (dressy or sporty), color (as specific as you can get), and if you want a solid, a stripe or a plaid pattern.

Now, pick out a shirt, tie, shoes and socks for that hypothetical suit, and wear them with your best-fitting, most comfortable suit while you're shopping. Don't be concerned if the colors or patterns of your shopping ensemble don't match.

When you try on suits in a store, you'll have a clearer idea of how the one you select will look as you actually plan to wear it if you dress for the occasion. Also, you can compare the fit of any suit you're considering with the comfortable one you're wearing.

Another point. Carry whatever objects you normally do in your jacket and pants pockets.

Now you're ready to go shopping.

When you arrive at the store, describe precisely what you have in mind to the sales clerk. After he has shown you the selection in your size, inform him that you'd like to look the suits over more closely by yourself. He'll probably grimace, but you keep smiling. Insist on your privacy if you have to. Resisting may be hard, but don't look at the price tags. Give any of the suits you like a quality check instead. Try on a jacket or two if you want to. Transfer your usual pocket-fillers into the trial jacket. (By now the salesman is likely turning green.) If a jacket doesn't fit fairly correctly across the shoulders and about the chest, or if it isn't within fractions of an inch of the correct length, discount it out of hand. These alterations are too costly and too unpredictable. If there is any jacket you especially like after trying it on, see what it costs. Even if it seems a bargain, don't buy it. Wave goodby to the bereft salesman and move on to another store. There, excuse yourself from the clerk once more and repeat your routine, looking for a suit style similar to the one you liked at the first store. Try the jacket on. Check the price tag.

It's a mistake to look at a price tag before you truly look at a suit, because knowing a price always colors our opinion of something's worth. A wise shopper first decides if he wants a particular item, then judges its affordability. Besides, visual comparison shopping is as important for dressing right as price comparisons.

After you have traumatized the sales forces of several stores by refusing their help, return to the store that has the suit you now know for certain that you want. Decency suggests that you look for the clerk who approached you on your previous sojourn, but if he flees, don't pursue. Tell any interested sales person that you want the suit.

Most stores have their own tailors, hopefully competent. But you may have to be firm. When you put your carry-alls in the pockets for fitting, refuse to remove them when the tailor asks you to. Gently let him know that you always carry these items, that you'll be carrying them inside the suit pockets when you wear the suit, so it's pointless to have the jacket or pants altered as if you aren't a pocket-filler. Also, when he tells you to stand straight, kindly inform him that you're going to remain in your usual posture.

"Too many men assume unnatural poses when trying on outfits before a mirror," notes Luciano Franzoni. "They become Napoleons posing for posterity, especially if they are the familiar 'concave chest/convex belly' types trying for that one moment to reverse what years of laziness and an addiction to munchies have produced."

The designer suggests that the average fellow's futile attempts to suck in the abdomen and expand the thorax by deep-breathing exercises last only as long as his interval before the mirror. "Soon our man looks like a bagpipe at rest again. As bad as it might be for his ego, if he'd insist to the fitter that, for better or worse, he stands like a deflated bagpipe and should be fitted accordingly, the fitter would be in the position to mark the proper corrections on the cloth," Franzoni notes. "Otherwise, the suit looks made for someone else."

An even better solution, of course, would be for the man to shape himself and his posture up. He'd be healthier, could remedy the perennial backaches that plague slouches and would look better. But that's too easy—or too hard.

Franzoni goes on to point out that men should become acquainted with their own posture problems, do something about them or accept them, and then explicitly ask a suit fitter to consider one of the classical alterations corresponding to bad posture. With a round back, the jacket becomes shorter at the back, so the front of the jacket may have to be shortened. Conversely, with a sway back, the jacket may need shortening in back. And if one shoulder is lower than the other, the jacket must be totally rebalanced to fit properly.

"It's always the jacket half of a suit or sports ensemble that gets special attention," Franzoni says, "but the proper fit for trousers or slacks is just as vital. Trousers are meant to cover our bodies from the waist down and, if we wish, to show the curves (and bulges) that Mother Nature gave us. But there's no reason why, with the help of a good tailor, we can't camouflage the curves and bulges we wish Mother Nature hadn't given us."

The designer offers three ideas for fellows with lower-figure problems. Bowlegged? Wear wide trousers. Trousers can be altered, moving the crease toward the inside of the pant leg, thus minimizing the "arch" effect. Knock-kneed? Don't wear baggy trousers. These men should have the crease moved to the outside, Franzoni suggests, de-emphasizing the "triangle" effect. Short legs? Don't wear wide pants which give a boxy look. The jacket for this type of man shouldn't be too long, thus permitting him to show as much trouser area as possible for a leggier appearance.

It's been suggested that, to get the best out of a fitter, the smart customer will slip a five in an unoutstretched palm before the measuring begins. Well, if someone wants to pass out fins right and left, so be it; but the odds are this generous guy won't get a better fit than if he talks honestly and plainly to a fitter. Any fellow should make it clear that he knows his needs and that he expects results. A straightforward heart-to-heart chat will talk louder than dough: no fitter wants an altered suit refused due to botched alterations. Besides, it's gauche to try to bribe haberdashers.

One last point. If you insist upon being fitted correctly, when you go back to pick up the suit, *try it on* to be certain the job was done right. If you don't have time that day to check out the job in the store's mirror, then you don't have the time to pick up the suit either.

CARE PACKAGE

Taking great pains to select the right clothes adds up to a bust if the clothes aren't adequately cared for. A filthy shirt is still a filthy shirt, whatever its original price tag or however handsome the fabric once was.

A smart buyer considers care and maintenance factors before purchasing. All-cotton shirts, certainly cooler and more comfortable than all-synthetics or natural-synthetic blends, wrinkle more easily and require ironing, thus raising laundry bills. Cream-colored suits show soilage more obviously than dark tweeds, thus increasing dry cleaning bills. Keeping shoes properly polished not only improves their appearance but extends their livelihood.

SUITS

Since suit and sport jackets are tailored three-dimensionally, they should always be hung on wooden or plastic *wishbone hangers,* the ones with some curvature to approximate the slope of the human shoulders and back. Jackets will not only maintain their shape better when hung on these fellows, but they will wrinkle less than if placed on the usual wire variety. Jamming jackets in a closet too tightly will cause wrinkling and present another problem—lack of breathing space. Jackets should have the opportunity to air out any body odors and consequently should always be given at least a twenty-four hour breather between wearings. When hung, they should not be buttoned and all articles in the pockets should be removed.

Suit trousers—actually, trousers of any kind—should preferably be hung on specially designed pants hangers that clamp onto the bottoms of the pants. This helps maintain the vertical crease. To avoid any tell-tale horizontal indentations on the trouser bottoms, you can fold a paper towel crosswise and sandwich it between the pants' fabric and the hanger. Remove belts before hanging; their weight can distort the lines of the trousers and add wrinkles. Don't overload the hangers; it destroys its spring-load mechanism.

Too frequent dry cleaning does suits no good. Periodically steam them behind closed doors in the bathroom with very hot water running to steam up the joint. But don't overdo. The steam can condense on the ceiling, releasing droplets of water and ruining your paint job. Five minutes or so is sufficient. But always have suits cleaned before seasonal storage. And get rid of those choking plastic bags immediately. Breathable cloth storage bags allow fibers to sustain themselves.

SHIRTS

Since shirts are most often worn next to the body where they come in direct contact with perspiration, shirts should be worn only once and then laundered. Starch takes a heavy toll on fabrics; shirts last longer if unstarched. They can either be folded neatly and piled, or they may be hung on hangers. Wire hangers risk rust stains, so plastic ones are better. Short on plastic hangers? Cover wire ones with white tissue paper, not newspaper, the ink from which can stain.

TIES

When taking a tie off, don't yank or pull it apart; untie it, reversing the knotting steps. Ties are made to be perfectly balanced. (A quality check when buying one is to drape the tie over your first two fingers to see how it hangs. If there's the slightest swivel, it's not balanced correctly.) When you twist or otherwise torture them, ties show the wear and tear. After carefully removing them, ties should always be hung up immediately. Knit ties, however, should be rolled and stored in a drawer. Hanging will stretch them out of shape.

When stained or dirty, ties should be dry cleaned. Beware, though, because many otherwise reputable dry cleaners can literally destroy good ties. Tie specialists are safer and are usually listed in the Yellow Pages, a great resource. Look them up under "Cleaners & Dyers" and look for special advertisements.

SWEATERS

Most sweaters are pretty tough, requiring little special care other than an occasional trip to the dry cleaners. But don't hang them on hangers. Like knit ties, they'll lose their shape. However, though durable, they shouldn't be subjected to unnecessary abuse. They can lose some of their dimensional stability when carelessly pulled on and off.

COATS

Overcoats should receive the same care as suit or sport jackets. Unless they're suede or leather, of course. Yet, being naturally porous, leathers and suedes need to breathe too.

Air is good for hides, and that's what suede and leathers are, tanned animal skins. Keep such garments in a well-ventilated place and never in an airtight plastic bag. Allow rain or snow to dry at room temperature away from heat. Heat, not water as is commonly supposed, is the natural enemy of leather and suede. Heat that's too direct and hot turns wet hides into brittle, dry skins.

Concerning suede, most spots can be lifted and buffed away with a soft eraser, sponge or bristle brush. In case of discoloration, rub one section against the other. To keep the garment looking fresh, periodically brush lightly with a soft sponge. Actually, you're supposed to give suede garments a quick rubdown after every wearing with a dry rubber sponge, a soft bristle brush or clean terry toweling.

For leather garments, use a soft, damp cloth with a mild soap to clean, followed by a thorough once-over with a clean, barely damp cloth to remove any soap residue. Under normal conditions, properly cared for leather garments may never require professional cleaning, but suedes should be cleaned yearly, at the conclusion of the season's wearing. For more specific details, contact the Leather Cleaning Guild of America.

SHOES

Our feet literally keep us from falling on our faces, so shoes take a lot of hard knocks. To protect

them from the outset, new shoes should always be polished before their first outing. Thereafter, shoes also need breathers of a day or more between wearings. While they are resting, shoe trees should be inserted to help them retain their shape. Shoehorns fend off back breakdowns.

Depending upon how often they are worn, leather shoes should be cleaned with saddle soap on the average of once a month to get rid of surface grime and excess wax while simultaneously softening the leather. Shoes should generally be polished after every couple wearings.

Suede shoes require only a stiff-bristled brushing from time to time to rough up the nap, but sharp-teethed brushes can injure the suede finish.

Wet shoes, like wet suede or leather garments, should never be dried close to extreme heat. Instead, blot off any excess water with paper toweling, insert shoe trees and allow the shoes to dry naturally at room temperature. (Wadded and stuffed newspapers can replace the shoe trees in a pinch.) As soon as possible after they've dried, put the shoes on and walk their creaks out. A swipe of saddle soap and a dab of polish or a couple quick buffs with a brush (for leather and suede shoes respectively) should accomplish the necessary resuscitation.

DRESSING HAPPY

With the right clothes and the right care, all you need is the right frame of mind. Hopefully, you've already got it.

This section is subtitled "Asserting Yourself." Self-assertion in clothing shouldn't extend to defiance. Defiance takes loads of energy, often misspent energy.

Positive self-assertion invigorates, never drains. It's akin to the feeling you experience after a good workout at the gym. You've tested yourself, extended yourself, and you feel exhilarated.

Dressing right, once you've really exercised your clothing muscle, gives you that kind of rush and self-satisfaction. It feels good.

Go ahead. Shine.

BODY WORKS

TACTICAL PLOYS

ANY BODIES

In dressing right, it never hurts to have a mesomorphic athletic build. Choosing clothes is never a hassle. But walking down the street, how many perfect specimens are there? Clearly some clothes will work for your physique and some won't. Some of the looks you consider the most fashionable or the most personality-filled may be totally off-base for your physique.

Now comes the turning point. You can't suspend judgment any longer. (The book is drawing to its close.) You must now decide whether you want to look fashionable, stylish or right. Because, as should now be apparent (especially if you go over the "Premise" of this book again), dressing fashionably, stylishly and *right* are not the same thing.

If you want to be fashionable, the whole notion of somatotyping be damned, buy what's in fashion and trust your luck. Don't worry about your waist or hip dimensions. Keep your body healthy and dress to the nines of the moment.

If you want to be stylish, just keep repeating to yourself that *you*—no one else can—know the look for you. Adopt an attitude and don't swerve. If you think your look is to-the-manor-born, even if your roots are Brooklyn tenements, screw anybody who chides. You know you; project that self-image with conviction. With self-assurance you will forge your own sense of style. If you flounder once in a while, so be it. The world won't end.

But if you want to *dress right*—in clothes that make the most of what your physique has to offer—then analyze how some clothes can help you in going after the Ideal Norm and how others may throw you off the track.

THE STOCKY ENDOMORPH

SUITS

Since this fellow's abdominal region is more prominent than his chest and shoulders, to add topside stature his suit jacket should have a tailored, lightly padded shoulder but minimal waist suppression. A modified, single- or double-breasted British silhouette will help. Unfortunately for him, many British models have side-vented jackets, but he needs a center vent: one vertical slit is not as hip-broadening. But if the vent is too deep and the hips are too broad, the jacket may have a tendency to split open in the back. A nonvented suit jacket is another alternative.

SPORT COATS

Any of the flared styles, such as hacking jackets, are poorly adapted to this body type, since they add more apparent weight to the hips. Norfolk jackets, with their self-belts, aren't good either, since they draw attention to the waistline. Waist emphasis has as a corollary hip emphasis. Pocket treatments on the lower portion of the jacket should be understated, so bellows and patch

pockets are off limits. Slanting hacking pockets too. The best pockets are in the inset besom style, preferably unflapped.

To fill out the chest, moderate to wide lapels are effective, so long as they don't engulf the torso. Peaked lapels work far better than shawl lapels, which draw the eye downward in an uninterrupted descent, whereas the accent should be on upward mobility. Notched lapels are neutral.

SHIRTS

If the neck is squat, as is often the case on many stocky endomorphs, then the collar should be low, and the spread moderate to narrow. Medium to short collar points will keep the focus closer to the face and away from the underdeveloped chest. Tab collars, if not too high, will do the same, as will pin collars, with or without a collar pin. Contrast collars are another means to lift the onlooker's eye, but contrast plackets are a mistake, since they produce an arrowlike line straight to the waistline. Smooth French fronts add no unnecessary bulk. A semi-tapered or full-cut body will fit the frame more easily than a European fit, which could cramp the gut, pointing out its roundness. Textured fabrics like oxford cloth are more attention-getting (but quietly so) near the face—where the attention should go—than smoother broadcloth or smoothest voile. French cuffs should be avoided since more weighting is undesirable anywhere lower than the chest.

NECKWEAR

A wider tie will broaden the chest more than a narrow one. Skinny ties are definitely out. Foulard patterned ties are better than regimental stripes, although patterning is less significant than tie width. Homespuns, shantungs, knits and other textured fabrics keep interest uppermost. Since bulkier tie fabrics are in order, the traditional four-in-hand is better than a windsor knot, which could look like a noose. Moderate bow ties can work, but not with chipmunk cheeks. Scarf and cravat treatments, if they don't appear choking, are an upward assist.

VESTS

Since vests create a V-shaped frame for the face and are almost always slimming, the stocky endomorph can rely greatly on them. However, vests should be in either the same fabric as the suit or sport jacket or darker in color.

PANTS

Jodhpurs would be disastrous for the behind. Low-rise pants will make the hips hippier. Pleats inflate the waistline and hips even more. Uncuffed pants with plain fronts and straight legs are the preferred style. Pocket treatments should be minimal. Lightweight fabrics, such as serge and poplin, add less apparent volume than heavy-duty cavalry twills and whipcords. Fine flannels and saxonies are better than sturdier cheviots and tweeds.

In shorts, perhaps surprisingly, Jamaica lengths are better than Bermudas, because longer styles emphasize hip dimensions more than medium ones. Short shorts, though, will not work at all.

SWEATERS

Since the stocky guy's shoulders are on the narrow side, dropped and dolman shoulders would draw attention to the fact. Moderate collar treatments are uplifting. Turtlenecks, which fill out the neck at the expense of the shoulders, aren't especially good, unless the entire sweater is bulky. Bulk, in fact, is the word: more fully proportioned sweaters, whatever the style, are preferable. True, they do add bulk to the waist as well as the shoulders, but the shoulders need filling out even at the expense of the waistline. Long sweater styles are bad investments, however, because they broaden the hips too, the worst idea for the stocky endomorph. Waist-length is as far as sweaters should go, so nearly every type of cardigan is out.

OUTERWEAR

The endomorph doesn't want a flaring dress coat style but one with broadening power about the shoulders. A single-breasted chesterfield is a good solution, while a full balmacaan is a bad one. Wrap coats and heavy double-breasted styles add an unwanted extra layer of fabric around the middle. Any kind of belt emphasizes the waistline.

For casual coats, the same principles apply. Fur-, pile- or shearling-lined coats make the middle more expansive. Hudson Bay coats double up with their colorful horizontal stripes to broaden the hips. Duffel coats, especially those with toggle buttons, have a vertical emphasis because of the distinctive closure, and are thus helpful. Loden coats, though usually double-breasted, do a number with their yokes to build up the shoulder area.

In jackets, hip-length and hip-conforming ones are tricky. They work only if the top of the jackets are ample. Waist-length jackets are better.

SWIMWEAR

Very brief or bikini styles, never. Gym-styled trunks are far more flattering.

THE STRINGY ENDOMORPH

SUITS

Suits present a problem of delicate balance. Wearing an extremely fitted, shaped silhouette, the ecotmorph may accentuate his linearity. But if he wears a roomy sack suit, he may look like a sad sack. If the lapels are too narrow, he'll look thinner, but the same thing could happen if the lapels are too wide. Moderate lapels, just barely on the narrow side, will keep the underdeveloped chest from being dwarfed. The jacket shoulders can have light padding, but roped shoulders will make the stringy fellow look scrunched up on top. The suit silhouette popular in the 40s and resurrected in the late 70s—wider shoulder trimming to a fairly slender waist with hardly more than a hint of European waist suppression—is a good compromise if all lines of the suit are relatively soft. This silhouette, sometimes called the *wedge,* imparts athleticism to the body. Peaked lapels are a bit much on this cut in particular and on the ectomorph in general. Notched lapels are more flattering, especially if the closure is low on the wedge. (Low closures, however, are a mistake on very trim silhouettes, since they lengthen, exactly what the ectomorph doesn't need, rather than broaden.) A wedge-cut jacket looks well nonvented. On a stringy physique, any other jacket style should be side-vented. Single-breasted styles should have at least a two-button closure. Double-breasted models can be fastened on the lowest button, if the jacket is not in a zoot suit length, to create a more triangular line on the torso and to broaden the shoulders, particularly on wedge-cut jackets.

SPORT JACKETS

The wedge silhouette is good on sport jackets too. A different alternative is slouchier, unstructured jackets that lend themselves to layering. Easier in construction, these styles soften the linear lines of a stringy ectomorph's body. Bel-lows, patch and flapped pockets all disrupt excessive angularity as well, while proportioning out the jacket's exterior.

SHIRTS

Stringy bodies are almost always accompanied by stringy necks which look best in high collars. However, the points should not be very long or they will add vertical emphasis. Rounded collars are one alternative. Medium collars with a moderate spread are another and are in balance with the moderate lapels of jackets in the wedge silhouette. Starkly contrasting collars draw too much attention to the neck. And contrast plackets slice the thin body into two thinner pieces. Stitched placket fronts add a bit more body to the frame. So do French cuffs, although they also lengthen long arms. A semitapered body, if not too full, will detract from some of the scrawniness. Otherwise, this style will compound the effect and should be bypassed for a shirt with a nonsevere European fit. Full-cut shirts never work. Oxford cloth, which looks right on all bodies other than hefty ones, is a good fabric choice. Handkerchief linen shirts fill out with their texture and are good adjuncts to unstructured jackets.

NECKWEAR

Skinny ties do the same thing that contrast plackets do, make the stringy ectomorph look skinnier. So do bright ties, since conventional ties are linear to begin with, and brights always hog the spotlight. Neckwear should initiate some widening action without becoming too conspicuous. Too wide ties will look like napkins on this body type. Moderately narrow ties, knotted in half-windsors, are likely bets. Bow ties with some bloom do a good job. Cravats and scarves are fine if they drape softly, not if they look uptight.

VESTS

Suit-matching vests almost always slenderize, and so are wrong for the very slender ectomorph. Contrasting vests in lighter colors and heavier textures help expand a nonemphatic torso.

PANTS

Dress and casual pants should probably be in two different styles. If the suit or sport jacket is somewhat wedge-shaped, to correspond to that silhouette, the accompanying trousers should be rather full at the top, possibly pleated, and either straight legged or moderately pegged. Thus, an overall wedge is formed. The same holds if the casual jacket is roomy and unstructured. On the other hand, casual pants worn without jackets will look better with a moderate flare. Repeat: moderate, not pronounced. Cuffs are optional but can't hurt. Heavier woolens are better than finer worsteds. Wide wale corduroy, uncut velvets, brushed denim, in addition to all twilled and corded fabrics, round out the body from the waist down.

Shorts are better when fuller or shorter or both. True, the legs will appear longer, hopefully not too much thinner, but it's preferable to look long-legged than merely long.

SWEATERS

Again, there are two prime possibilities—skinny or bulky—and then some. (In general, a slender person has more clothing options than a stocky one.) If pants are cut fully, the top can look skinny without suggesting that the stringy ectomorph is starving. It's a look. So is combining bulky tops with skinny bottoms in a long-legged routine. Or bulky tops with rather full bottoms. However, skinny top with skinny bottom on skinny frame is the cardinal ectomorphic sin. Although no shortage of available sweaters exists for the stringy male, some styles are easier or harder to work with. Easier: boat necks; collar necks; cowl necks; raglan shoulders; bouclé and other bumpy knits; cable knits; fisherman's sweaters. Harder: henley necks; mock turtles; scoopnecks; dropped shoulders; set-in shoulders; some flat, plain or rib knits.

OUTERWEAR

The ratio of length to flare is the major consideration. A very long topcoat with a pencil-thin silhouette will make the stringy ectomorph appear a giant pencil himself. But a flaring style terminating at the knees might suggest that he couldn't find a coat long enough to fit him. Below-the-knee, tailored, double-breasted styles are wise investments. A belted polo coat with large flapped patch pockets is another sterling choice. Indeed, belted coats in general inject an appreciated horizontal element. Overlapping wrap coats help cover up the ectomorphy. Sturdy balmacaans, if not too generous, likewise do the trick. Much-detailed trench coats, generous greatcoats and rich fur coats can be worn most easily on this type

frame. As mentioned, the slender male has more options than the guy with more girth.

In casual coats, the choices remain large, although car coats in general don't quite make it. Duffel, Hudson Bay, loden, melton, ranch and sweater coats usually do.

SWIMWEAR

Extreme styling, either in brevity or volume, should be passed by. In a bikini, the body will appear more underfed. In a boxer trunk, thin legs will stick out like stilts. Standard suits like racers make no excuses.

THE Y-SHAPED ENDO/ECTOMORPH

SUITS

First of all, this fellow has a rough go of it buying suits that fit him. With his wide top and narrow bottom, his mismatched physique hardly ever corresponds to conventional suit sizes, and the fact offers him a clue: he's better off in sport jackets and trousers.

SPORTJACKETS

Since this Y-shaped guy is unsuited for suits, a navy blue blazer has high priority. Peaked lapels have no priority at all. Moderate to narrow lapels stop his expansive chest from expanding further. Shawl lapels are better than too skinny ones, which conspire to imply he's a schoolboy outgrowing his jacket. No shoulder padding whatsoever is called for. Waist suppression, if any, should be understated, since the waistline and hips are already too minor in the physical composition. Surprisingly, double-breasted jackets, which usually add some bulk to the torso (which presumably this guy doesn't need), can be very effective in reapportioning this mismatched body if the style is four-button with a low closure and if the fabric is lightweight to medium. In single-breasted jackets, though, the closure should be higher, maybe even a three-button version, so the framed shirt exposure is played down. A man with this physique in exaggeration has difficulty carrying off unstructured jackets, since they may hang like smocks. Unpronounced Y-shapes, conversely, look good in them without bundled-up layers which defeat the whole purpose.

SHIRTS

If possible, the best shirt collar is relatively high, with long points and a narrow spread, since it lengthens and consequently slenderizes the top of the chest. However, some Y-shaped endo/ecto-morphs have bullish necks, and high collars on them could conjure visions of no-neck monsters. In that case, the collar should be low, but still have longish points with a narrow spread. Tapered bodies make the Y-shape appear more extreme. Semitapered fits with French fronts smooth out the proportions somewhat by adding some full-ness to the receding waistline. French cuffs aren't a bad idea, although they're seldom worn with sportier jackets. Batiste, broadcloth, voile and smooth fabrics are the best; chambray the worst.

NECKWEAR

A Y-shaped man should beware of bow and wide ties. Cravats and scarves are also dubious, as are most uplifting notions. Narrowish ties with diagonal weaves are better than wider ones with a crosswise grain. Rough-woven homespuns and knit or crochet ties with their irregular surfaces are to be avoided. Neckwear with small patterns make the right understatement.

VESTS

Overall, vests slenderize, but the Y-shaped man wants to trim only his chest measurements while filling out his waist and hips. Thus, some vests work, others don't. Vests with low closures accentuate the Y, so they are out. The same is true of vests with lapels. Higher-buttoning vests confine the triangular appearance of the shirt and thus are better. What really matters is how much Y-shape the physique carries. With loads of it, vests are seldom a good idea, since any type of layering is overwhelming.

PANTS

Stopping short of elephantine bells, this fellow can get away with, and probably requires, widish, straight-legged or flared pant styles. He should avoid Western-cut jeans and pegged legs except with the most casual outfits, when he might choose to look leggy. Low-rise pants are never advisable. His pants should always be belted, usually pleated and cuffed if he chooses. Like the ectomorph (since that's the basic conformation of his body from the waist down), he should veer toward sturdier and

heftier fabrics: cavalry twills, cheviots, chinos (heavy ones), corduroys, herringbones, khakis, tweeds, velvets and whipcords.

In shorts, mid-length to longer versions with full-cut legs are the right choices. Sizable pocket treatments are likewise preferable to dainty ones.

SWEATERS

Bulk is bad. Flat is fine. V-necks with set-in shoulders are outstandingly the best choice. Less good, but not really bad, are turtlenecks, mock turtles, ring or henley or keyhole necks. Scandinavian ski sweaters, sweaters with dolman, dropped or raglan shoulders are wrong styles. Sweaters should be as simple as possible.

OUTERWEAR

Coats should also be in the simple vein. Relatively nondescript reefer coats are more flattering than coats with elaborate detailing. Epaulets and shoulder yokes pile extras on the extra-proportioned shoulders. Period coats, questionable on most physiques, are hardest to wear by endo/ectomorphs. Greatcoats aren't much easier. Nor are wrap coats. Double-breasted coats may or may not go; the most likely to succeed are straight-hanging or subtly-shaped, such as a below-the-knee British warm.

Concerning casual coats, simplicity still applies. Another general guideline: the shorter the coat, the more difficulty. Hudson Bay coats are exceptions. Even though they are hefty and only thigh-touching, the colorful stripes encircling their bottoms help by adding volume to the hip area. But bold blanket coats and mackinaws have too much going on and cause the Y-shaped fellow to appear more top-heavy.

Jackets aren't easy either. If the pants are amply cut, blouson and drawstring jackets may perform the balancing feat. Shirt jackets are more tailored than sweater jackets, so the former are better than the latter. Parkas, battle and bomber jackets can make even a moderately Y-shaped individual appear barrel-chested.

SWIMWEAR

High-waisted boxer trunks, though hardly anyone's favorites, are the most visually acceptable. Leg-conforming jams are the least, although they receive serious competition from bikinis.

THE PEAR-SHAPED ECTO/ENDOMORPH

SUITS

Like the endo/ectomorph, who is mismatched in the opposite way, the pear-shaped fellow also has problems when it comes to suits. If the suit jacket fits, the trousers don't. He might resort to portly sizes but would probably have more to choose from in sport jackets and dress pants. Similar to the body proportions of the typical endomorph, although given to exaggeration, this somatotype is better suited to American than British silhouettes. However, natural-shoulder garments give him problems: he may require heavily padded, though not engineered, shoulders. On the other hand, since his waistline is larger than his chest, waist suppression is out. His body is a hybrid, so his suit style should be also. But hybrid suits aren't easy to find; especially without many costly alterations, reaffirming the pear-shaped guy's dependence on sport coats and slacks.

SPORTCOATS

Country and tweed jackets, because of the ruggedness of the fabrics, do more for this body configuration than finely tailored models. Self-belted styles are dangerous. Worse are hacking jackets or even hacking pockets, since the flare and the slant only reinforce the pear shape. Oddly, narrow lapels work, creating an optical illusion of more chest expansion. These lapels may throw other elements of the outfit into individual imbalance, but an overall balance is the desired end. The jacket closure and length should both be on the longish side, to give a long-line look to the silhouette, another reason to opt for narrow or shawl lapels. Consequently, single-breasteds win out over double-breasted models.

SHIRTS

Trying to add dimension to his torso, the pear-shaped man is better off in a low collar with a wide spread and medium points. Short points will stunt his upper half more than genetics did. Pin and tab collars are poor. So are contrast collars. Clean lines look better than complicated ones on this framework; French and fly front shirts don't shout for attention. Oxford cloth shirts are fine with a vest; unvested, broadcloth is better. French cuffs do nothing but drag the eye to the hips.

NECKWEAR

With narrow lapels on the jacket, narrow neckwear (or a bow tie) is called for. The suggested collar style has a wide spread and medium points, which usually is accompanied by a relatively wide tie. The solution is to tie the narrow tie in a fullish knot, to localize the bulk in the knot and not in the tie's width. Horizontal or diagonal stripes, plus weaves with a crosswise grain, help balance the could-be imbalance between the tie and the collar. Big scarf treatments look out of place; controlled ones don't.

VESTS

Since a vest draws the eye to the upper torso while trimming the lower portion, a vest in the same tone and fabric as the suit or sport jacket helps keep the focus higher up. If the jacket is worn buttoned, a slightly lighter colored vest, though precarious if poorly executed, may serve handsomely.

PANTS

Even though the advice for the endo/ectomorph (the exact opposite of this pear-shaped fellow) is to stay clear of pegged pants, the same advice is underscored for the ecto/endomorph. In pegged pants, his Y-shaped counterpart would come on as an inverted triangle, whereas our pear-shaped friend would come off as the personification of a baseball diamond. That's the crux of his problem: while he should compensate for the amplified waist and hips, when he overcompensates to strike a supposedly proper balance, the balance looks improper. He's ruled more by what he shouldn't do than by what he should. He shouldn't wear wide bells. He shouldn't wear even moderate flares. He shouldn't wear Western jeans. He shouldn't wear contrasting belts. He shouldn't wear patch or bellows or any exposed pockets. What's left? Medium-rise, plain-front, straight-leg pants with inset pockets and with a self-waistband. Not exactly handed a wide selection, he is also well advised to bypass twilled or tweedy pant fabrics. Worsted, serges, lightweight chinos, saxonies and poplins are his best bets.

Shorts are no bed of roses. Heavy fabrics are out. Bermudas won't be a joy to behold, but they'll look better than hot pants.

SWEATERS

What he lacks in breadth of choice in pants, the pear-shaped man can sort of make up for in sweaters. Although wrap and peasant sweaters pose problems, waist-stopping styles don't. Crewnecks, turtlenecks, V-necks and shawl collars may be a little better than other styles.

OUTERWEAR

Back to limitations. Double-breasted, wrap and belted styles do nothing to improve his physique. Neither do full cuts like the balmacaan. Exposed pocket treatments continue the negativity. Reefer coats and single-breasted chesterfields are two positives.

Casual coats have a little more leeway. One wouldn't think it, but sturdy loden and duffel coats, with their purposeful bulk, help make the pear-shaped man appear more purposeful. Shoulder yokes and hoods proportion out the top of the torso. Car, ranch, stadium and car coats aren't necessarily bad. Those with moderately large collars are favored.

Collars also help on jackets. Baseball jackets are inappropriate. Bomber and other waist-length and waist-fitting jackets fill out the top without encumbering the hips with extra bulk. Parkas and lumberjack jackets are toss-ups. Some are okay, if enough is going on atop.

SWIMWEAR

Boxer trunks will look voluminous, bikinis like Band-Aids. Standard-sized swimwear or the athletic-inspired variety are the least jarring.

THE ROTUND BUILD

SUITS

If the guidelines seem few, that's because there's not much a rotund fellow can do to disguise his rotundity. Sack suits, though he may look like a sack of potatoes, are the choice for the round body. You can't suppress a jacket's waist if there's no waist suppression on the frame. Maybe the shoulder can be slightly built up. Center vents are less broadening than side ones. Lapels should be moderate. In fact, with this body configuration, every clothing aspect should be in moderation. Double-breasted styles will look immoderately much. Although proper fit is always important, it's absolutely crucial on a rotund physique.

SPORT JACKETS

As with suits, the choice of sport jackets is primarily a matter of what the man can fit himself into, which doesn't leave a lot of room. He'll find the best selection in shops catering to big and tall men. Nevertheless, if he sees a stunning tweed or a marvelous plaid, he should pass. Ostentatious styles look like circus tents on his frame. The only appropriate pockets are inset minus flaps. Fabrics should never be more than medium-weight.

SHIRTS

Wide spread collars rival with rounded collars for the prize as the most detracting style. A medium to low collar with longish points and a narrow spread wins hands down as the best. French fronts are called for; French cuffs aren't. Contrast collars, cuffs and plackets are too attention-grabbing. Broadcloth is better than oxford cloth. Chambray shirts should never be worn. White on white patterns add more when less is wanted. Knit shirts bulge with the bulges.

NECKWEAR

Neither narrow nor wide widths are acceptable. To repeat, moderation. Even pointed club bow ties look too stylized.

VESTS

A good marriage.

PANTS

Take a look at all the don'ts mentioned in pant styles for pear-shaped men. They are the same warnings, only with doubly negative emphasis, for rotund men. No-anything pants with extension waistbands are the only right wearables.

SWEATERS

Naturally, there are far more sweater styles that can't be worn than those that can. Sticking to classic V-necks is the best route. Square necks and boat necks are worth exploring, but wraps and belted cardigans are too adventurous. All textured knits, with the possible exception of understated ribs, are too far off the beaten path. Any highly patterned numbers offer roads not to be taken. Here's that word again, moderation. Subtlety or understatement could replace it.

OUTERWEAR

It comes as no jolt that the choices are limited. No double-breasted overcoats. No flaring coats. No any style except the most unobtrusive. Of course, if a rotund man wants to have a fling with a fur coat, who's to stop him?

Casual coats and jackets should also recede as far as possible into neutrality.

SWIMWEAR

The only body around that is best covered by cabana sets (preferably not in Hawaiian prints), rotund frames should expose as little skin as possible.

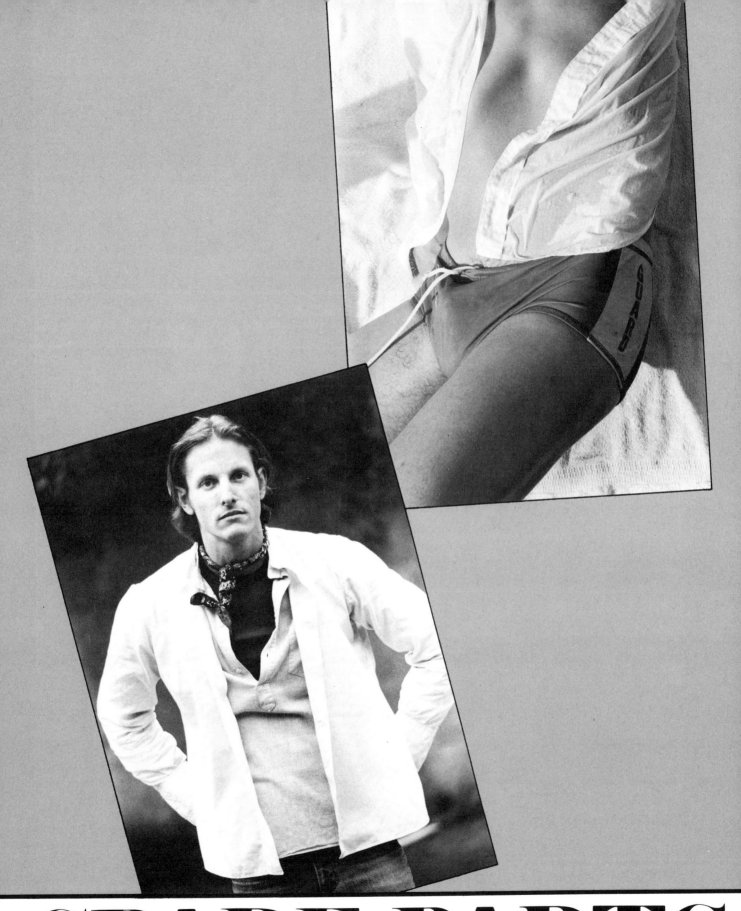

SPARE PARTS

CLOTHES LINES

ALL ABOUT SUITS & SPORT JACKETS

By definition, a suit is nothing more complicated than an outfit consisting of a jacket and trousers, with or without a vest, sometimes called a waistcoat. Traditionally, though not necessarily, the jacket and trousers are made of the same fabric.

Construction refers to shoulder padding and other manufacturing processes that add engineered, three-dimensional shape to a suit jacket, whether the steps are done by hand or machine. *Unconstructed* jackets are those without shoulder padding and often without any lining; when hanging limply, they resemble shirts more than tailored jackets. *Semiconstructed, deconstructed, décontracté, unstructured* and *soft-constructed* suits (no one is sure what to call them) are somewhere between the other unconstructed and traditionally tailored ones.

Some people say that unconstructed suits aren't suits at all but sportswear. Others extend this mental rigidity to semiconstructed, deconstructed, unstructured and soft-constructed suits. Who cares? Unconstructed suits by their very nature are less "suit-y" than conventional suits. So are the semi-, de-, un- and soft- varieties. The point is, they are jacket-and-trouser outfits. So

are safari suits, which don't look like conventional suits either. Leisure suits, which many people prefer to pretend never existed, are also suits, if only by virtue of their given name.

Conventional suits are first differentiated by cut or silhouette, basically interchangeable terms referring to a suit's outline. The jacket is the point of comparison.

THE AMERICAN CUT

It has not-too-wide, only lightly padded or unpadded shoulders, so that the fabric conforms to the shoulders of the man wearing the garment, giving rise to the phrase *natural shoulder* clothing. The jacket is usually straight-hanging, allowing a comfortable, natural fit. Waist suppression (tailored-in-shaping) is totally or nearly nonexistent. Sometimes called a *sack suit,* it is almost always center-vented. The Ivy-styled, three-button, narrow-lapeled suit is an example of the American cut.

THE EUROPEAN CUT

Most people think of this cut as being slimmer in its proportions, with padding in the shoulders to impart a built-up look, variously referred to as *high, squared, pitched* or *roped shoulders.* The waist is suppressed, either a little or a lot, creating a shaped silhouette. The shaping has tended to become more relaxed in recent years since it was

first introduced and popularized by Pierre Cardin. Today many American manufacturers are cutting models in the European cut, and the styles have been adapted to the American male's physique.

Another European look—*décontracté*—that emerged in the latter 70s is characterized by the softer, deconstructed approach, a more avant garde look of unpadded, often unlined jackets with a tossed-off insouciance. Hard to pin down, this look is more attitudinal than specific.

THE BRITISH CUT

This is less a particular silhouette than a fabricated image, either that of the well-tailored-suit-with-derby or country-tweeds. The jackets, often midpoint between their American and European counterparts, have restrained shaping and usually are side-vented.

SINGLE-BREASTED SUITS

These have only one vertical line of buttons on the jacket. Those with two or three buttons are the more typical, although some jackets have only one button. More faddish—and infrequent—styles have four and even five. When the jacket has more than one button, the lower one most often is not fastened, not so much as a style consideration, but because that can kill the architectural balance of the garment. Where the buttons are situated in relationship to the torso is called the *closure* or *button stance.* A lower closure is closer to the waist, permitting more shirt or vest to show.

DOUBLE-BREASTED SUITS

These overlap for some inches in the front of the jacket, with two rows of vertical buttons. There may be two, four or six buttons, seldom if ever more, with one row merely decorative. In six-button models, sometimes the top two are more widely spread and not in line with the bottom four. In this case, no attempt should be made to fasten the top button, since it really isn't functional. Time was when rules dictated that all buttonable buttons on a double-breasted jacket should be fastened. With the collapse of the fashion dictatorship, personal choice and flair became the determinants of where and how—or even whether—to button a double-breasted jacket. Current styles are often made with a lower, bottom-button closure.

THE LAPELS

Conventional, and unconventional for that matter, suits have *lapels,* the front folds of fabric that are turned back at the jacket's opening from the collar downward. Lapel widths vary with the cut of the suit and its overall proportions. Wider lapels are traditionally worn with more ample shirt collars and wider ties.

THE NOTCHED LAPEL. This has an angled V-shaped opening at the point where the collar of the jacket meets the lapel.

THE PEAKED LAPEL. On the other hand, here is an upward slanting lapel, coming to a point (peak), leaving only a narrow space between the collar and the lapel.

THE SHAWL LAPEL. Without a notch or a peak to its name, this lapel has a continuous collar that slopes down in a curve to the suit's top-button closure.

Distinguishing what is a sport coat or jacket from what isn't can be puzzling. One thing a sport jacket isn't is a suit coat worn with an odd pair of trousers, although the masquerade can be undetectable.

THE BLAZER. It is probably the most classic sport jacket. The term blazer can be traced to the 1860s when a British captain of the H.M.S. *Blazer* looked disdainfully on his dishevelled crew and shouted for a tailor, who whipped up identical metal-buttoned blue serge jackets for the motley sailors.

Some purists insist that metal buttons make the difference between blazers and non-blazers, but even pearl and horn buttons have been worn on what most would call legitimate blazers. The name first conjures the color navy blue, but the blazer can be striped or checked. Tartan plaid and madras blazers keep the name. Blazers can be single- or double-breasted and come in any silhouette, with notched, peaked or shawl lapels.

CHESTERFIELD JACKETS. These sport jackets, made along the lines of the chesterfield overcoat but drastically shortened to sport-jacket length, most often have the standard velvet collar,

although the jacket lapels match the body fabric. Otherwise they can be single- or double-breasted in any silhouette, but most often are cut along the lines of the British style in the body with natural shoulders.

COUNTRY JACKETS. Loosely lumped together by appearing outdoorsy even when found

indoors, country jackets can be fine *harris tweeds* (those woven by hand on the islands of the Outer Hebrides) or warm and lightweight *Shetlands* (made with Shetland yarns from Scotland) or rugged corduroys, among other fabrications. Some have matching or contrasting elbow patches, throat latches and other similar details. They primarily suggest a British look, since they were originally worn by the landed gentry on their estates.

HACKING JACKETS. One form of country sport coat, hacking jackets were first designed for horseback riding. They are shaped with a longer than ordinary waist, flared over the hips, and have deep center- or side-vents for comfort in the saddle. Naturally, some men who wear contemporary versions have never been within spitting distances of a horse.

THE NORFOLK JACKET. This is another country-jacket variation. When introduced, it was pleated on each side, front and back, with an all-around belt of matching fabric stitched to the jacket on its front and sometimes on its back. Having survived many reinterpretations, it is now more a generalized look, exemplified by the attached self-belt, than a precisely cut garment.

POCKET TREATMENTS

THE BELLOWS POCKET. This is definitely one of the more sporty pocket treatments. It has folds or pleats around the three sewn sides, so the pocket is somewhat expandable. It's usually topped with a flap, sometimes one that buttons. The pocket initially was adapted to hunting and

shooting for extra carrying space. It is also called a *saddlebag pocket* when a button-down flap is present.

THE BESOM POCKET. It's a "hidden" pocket, meaning the pocket is inset within the garment with only a slash opening. Both edges of the slit have narrow stitched folds (welts) along the seams or edges.

THE FLAPPED POCKET. Any type of pocket that is overhung with a flap. A flapped besom pocket would have a corresponding welt seam across the top of the flap.

THE HACKING POCKET. Typically found on hacking jackets, this style is sewn on a slant and is most often flapped.

THE INSET POCKET. Sometimes called a *slashed* or *slash pocket,* one version is the besom pocket, but inset pockets don't necessarily have welt seams. They also may or may not be flapped.

THE PATCH POCKET. Made of the garment's fabric and sewn to the outside of the garment, it literally appears to be a patch.

THE TICKET POCKET. This is a small pocket, with or without a flap, found above the regular right-hand pocket of the jacket. An extra convenience as well as a styling detail, the ticket pocket is sometimes called a *change pocket.*

ALL ABOUT SHIRTS

It's not always easy to say what a dress shirt is, other than a shirt supposedly designed to be worn with a jacket and tie. In practice, dress shirts often express themselves more freely.

Once dress shirts were sold by specific neck and sleeve sizes, while sport shirts came in small, medium and large. With the dubious advent of average sleeve lengths, that distinction no longer applies. Also less distinctly apparent is the differentiation between dress and casual patterns. Plaids, tattersalls and checks are common to both dressy and sporty shirts.

THE COLLAR

The most important aspect of a dress versus a sport shirt is its collar. Although the gradations of differences are not especially easy to spot, a vocabulary of collar terms exists to help draw the distinctions.

The *spread* of the collar refers both to the distance between the two sides of the collar where it is fastened by the collar button, and also to the spacing at the bottom between the two tips. Each separate section is termed a *point,* which sounds easy enough, but each final point of the collar is also called a *point,* and the distance from the top of the collar to the tip is likewise described as the *point,* or sometimes the *cape,* less frequently the *rise.*

For simplicity, most people refer to the depth of the collar tips or points in descriptive terms. That is, collars have long, medium or short points, translating into long, medium or short collars. Similarly, spreads have varying widths, from narrow to wide, so a wide-spread collar is precisely that, although the points can be short or long.

Collars are also said to be high or low. A collar's

height or lack of it (sometimes called its *slope*) is determined by the depth of the *collarband* (also called the *neckband*), that strip of fabric sewn to the top of the shirt which holds the collar button and buttonhole, and to which the collar is joined. In most cases, the height of the collar should correspond to the length of the neck: Lower collars on shorter necks, higher collars on longer necks, although other factors should also be considered.

THE BUTTON-DOWN COLLAR. Aptly named, this style has buttons on the body of the shirt and buttonholes at the collar points through which the buttons are fastened. Considered a classic and conservative collar, the button-down, while connoting the Ivy League way of dressing, has more modes than one might guess. It can rest relatively flat or it can have a *roll*, a slight flare. Usually, the shorter the points, the flatter they rest above the collar bones. Button-downs are never truly out of style although they may be cyclically out of mass favor.

THE LONG-POINT COLLAR. Again, the name conveys a fair amount of information, since

this collar style has characteristic long points. Not specified in the name is that the distance between the points is relatively narrow, so "narrow-spread" could be tacked on to refine the basic style further. Truthfully, long-point collars aren't all that long; they are the staples of collars, the most widely worn style. Really long long-points are faddish extremes, even though they may enjoy moments of glory and be worn by many. During the 30s a very popular style was the *Barrymore collar* with a low-set front and rakishly long points; the term is no longer used. A continuing long-point version is the *Hollywood roll collar,* a long and flaring style.

THE SPREAD COLLAR. Since all collars have a spread, this name is less descriptive. Essentially a spread collar is a wide-spread collar, most often with shortish points. The *windsor collar* (another defunct term buried with the 30s) had an extremely wide spread, to accommodate the sizable windsor knot popularized by the Duke

of Windsor. Relatively short collars with narrow spreads are sometimes called *pin collars,* since they are (or can be) worn with collar pins.

In addition to these three basics, there are other collar treatments, sometimes called fashion collars, the availability of which ride trendy and erratic waves.

THE SHAWL COLLAR. Introduced in America in the late 1970s, this style has a very narrow collar with sloping curves on either side of the neckband button. Smaller and less "tailored" than the French collar, it is generally worn with very narrow ties.

THE BAND COLLAR. This type shirt with no collar has several names and is seldom thought of as a true dress shirt, although it can be worn as one without a tie.

THE FRENCH COLLAR. It has slightly rounded points and may be called a *rounded collar* or a *continental collar*. Usually the cape measurement (saying "points" seems inappropriate when there are none) is rather short while the slope of the collar tends to be high. When shirts have enlarged rounded collars, perhaps so they can button down, they may cross the hazy borderline into becoming sport shirts.

THE TAB COLLAR. This style has points kept in place by fastening together the tabs that are sewn on the reverse sides of the points. The points tend to be pointedly short, the spread not too wide.

THE UNDERSIZED COLLAR. Of course, its designers would not consider it undersized, however, the definitely smaller collars of certain fashion-conscious shirts of the latter 70s do appear pint-sized in comparison to more conventional, though moderate, shirt collar styles.

CONTRAST COLLARS. They are not, strictly speaking, collar styles but represent a fashion look. Yes, the collars contrast with the body fabric of the shirt. A white collar on a blue-and-white striped shirt is a contrast collar. So would be a blue-and-white striped collar on a white shirt, although this combination is less likely to occur in dress shirts. Shirts with contrast collars may or may not have contrast cuffs.

THE BODY

Dress shirts or not, all shirts have bodies, that portion between the shoulders and the garment's tail. A tapering body, sometimes called the *European fit,* is darted rather severely so the fit of the shirt follows closely to the torso from shoulders to chest to waist, where it flares out again. The armholes are high and relatively close-fitting. Of course, if the torso itself lacks tapering, the shirt's buttons will pull and bulge.

Conversely, a *full-cut* body has no taper at all, so the dimensions are the same at the chest and waist and tail. Armholes are lower and looser. When a torso tapers but the shirt body is full-cut, the shirt may appear sloppy.

Semitapered fits are proportioned with casual darting for the average build.

Unfortunately, there is little or no uniformity in body contouring among shirtmakers, so the terms only hint at the actual fit.

A word about stitching. Many shirt seams are constructed with a double row of stitching at the seams, called *double-needle tailoring.* In *single-needle tailoring,* the seams are stitched first on the inside, then on the outside, resulting in a flatter, reinforced seam that makes the shirt conform more naturally to the body. A more expensive procedure, single-needle construction hikes the shirt's price tag.

Whatever the body style, all dress shirts have buttoned fronts.

THE PLACKET FRONT. This is a reinforced panel of fabric that's pleated back and stitched vertically, usually on both sides of the buttonholes.

THE FRENCH FRONT. This is smooth. The buttonholes are near the edge of the front with no additional stitching or details.

THE FLY FRONT. This is really a false front, with buttons hidden by an overlapping smooth placket. Often in the same fabric as the body of the shirt, fly fronts, and less often placket fronts, may be of contrasting fabric or color or both.

THE FABRICS

Dress shirt fabrics are usually made of natural fibers (cotton, silk, wool, et cetera) or natural/synthetic blends. Most often they are woven. Knit fabrics in shirts, though worn by some on dress occasions, are currently pretty much frowned on by the fashion-minded. Knitted shirts can be either single- or double-knits. The reverse side of *single-knits* looks unfinished, whereas the reverse side of *double-knits* looks just as correct as the front.

BATISTE. Shirts of this fabric are sheer and finely woven. Very lightweight, batiste is made in many fibers.

BROADCLOTH. Shirts of this fabric are closely woven in a fine, tight weave with a barely visible rib. The finish appears very soft and lustrous. Originally broadcloth only referred to cotton fabrics, but today broadcloth fabrics are made from many fibers.

CHAMBRAY. More used in casual than dress shirts, this lightweight cloth has a colored warp and a white filling thread. It is similar in appearance to denim but is much lighter. Chambray once meant only fabric woven from cotton, but no longer.

HANDKERCHIEF LINEN. Out of style for years, shirts of this fabric staged a comeback with designers late in the 70s. Traditionally, handkerchief linen was a very lightweight, extremely sheer fine linen. In shirtings, the fabric is a bit heavier, but the texture still resembles that of a linen handkerchief.

OXFORD CLOTH. Originally woven by a mill in Scotland as one of four fabrics named after the universities of Harvard, Yale, Cambridge and Oxford, today oxford cloth is the only one extensively used in shirtings. The fabric is a basket weave, often with colored vertical threads and white filling, combining heavy and fine yarns to produce a slight texture. Blends have invaded the territory first occupied only by fine cottons.

VOILE. Most often refers to a plain weave of cotton that produces a lightweight, crisp, sheer fabric.

WHITE-ON-WHITE. This fabric has a slightly raised pattern motif in white woven on a white background, producing the named effect.

ALL ABOUT PANTS

Pants were once a colloquialism for trousers, then became known as any inexpensive type of trouser, and now cover the whole spectrum of outer garments extending from the waist to below the knees and covering each leg separately (as opposed to a kilt). But even walking shorts or hot pants can loosely be considered pants.

THE STYLES

WESTERN. America's oldest fashion, true Western jeans are exemplified by only one look, that of denim jeans with straight legs and two front pockets (one with a change pocket above it) with angled entries. In their many incarnations, jeans are sometimes called Levis, dungarees or denims. Pants in fabric other than denim are often cut in jean styles.

CASUAL. They are just about anything imaginable. Often the fabrics employed, pocket treatments, and the use of stitching separately or collectively relegate trousers into a casual category.

DRESS. These are certified for wearing with sport jackets or dressy sweaters. Like the casual appellation, dress is mainly a matter of personal taste and social convention. What is designated solely as casual slacks in one region, community or household can be another's dress pants.

JODHPURS. These are a form of riding breeches. The pants are cut full above the knee, tight below, fitting closely to the cuffed ankle, sometimes with a strap passing under the boot to hold the jodhpurs in place.

KNICKERS. Another atypical style, knickers are also cut full above the knee, with that looseness extending to below the knee. Then and there, knickers are fastened with a band and a buckle instead of a cuff. *Plus fours,* worn widely during the 20s and 30s by golfers, are full-cut knickers that stop precisely four inches below the knee. Not seen on city streets daily, knickers are worn to be kicky, some might say kinky.

SHORTS

CUT-OFFS. These are shorts that were once trousers. Often the remains of old jeans, though they needn't be, and since they are individualized by scissor action, they can be almost crotch-high to knee-length. Technically, shorts stop being shorts when they pass below the knees.

ISLAND SHORTS. *Bermudas* reach nearly to the break of the knee. *Nassau Shorts* creep up to a slightly lower than midthigh length. *Jamaica Shorts* creep up higher.

HOT PANTS. They make the big leap, tightening severely around the thighs and groin.

WALKING SHORTS. These styles descend again to more conservative lengths. Possessing such a nonspecific name, they can be in Nassau or Jamaica lengths but may have add-on details like cargo pockets or deep cuffs and are usually of heavyish fabrics.

GYM SHORTS. Also called *athletic shorts,* they come in a variety of sports-influenced styles and are generally fairly short and loose. They may have the logo of one's own or imagined alma

mater. Some have ribbonlike trim sewn across the bottoms and up the sides. Or, shorts may be in a gym style simply by having an elasticized waist without the legs flaring appreciably. When very flared, they are *boxer shorts,* though not the kind worn as underwear.

SURFING SHORTS. They can masquerade as shorts or bathing/surfing attire. *Jams,* with their drawstring waists and longish lengths, though sometimes also worn for surfing or as resort casualwear, are in the limbo inhabited by surfing shorts.

ALL ABOUT SWEATERS

A funny thing about sweaters. We seldom think why they were named. The prosaic truth is that they began their fashion life as heavy woolen numbers worn for the express purpose of producing sweat. Later, they became abbreviated to sweatshirts. Now, although they can be worn for warmth, sweaters are as essential to the male wardrobe as shoes and socks. They do far more than energize the sweat glands. Sweaters do part-time duty as shirts, vests, sport jackets, coats, scarves (when tossed around the shoulders) and belts (when tied around the waist), which is pretty heavy-duty performing. They are also vital ingredients in layering, whether executed in the classical or attitudinal mode.

Sweaters come in only three basic versions: the *pullover,* which slips on over the head; the *cardigan,* which doesn't, but buttons, zips, snaps, wraps, belts or hangs instead; and the *vest,* which may be either a pullover or a cardigan but is always sleeveless and seldom is longer than waist-length.

NECKLINES

THE BOAT NECK. Supposedly this neck style, which is also found on casual shirts (as most

otherwise, carries some type of collar treatment, big or small, in the same color or weave or not.

THE COWL NECK. Some might call this an overgrown turtleneck. The neck opening is round but wider than most other sweaters. With a sizable extension of material atop the body, the neck of the sweater then folds over and drapes, sometimes falling below the collar line in front.

sweater necklines are), resembles a boat, in that the neck opening follows the curve of the collarbone in a horizontal slash, reaching almost from shoulder to shoulder.

THE CARDIGAN NECK. Although cardigan sweaters may have several other neck treatments, this so-named style covers two alternatives. One is a high, round neckline on a front-buttoning sweater. The other is the more traditional one associated with cardigans: the two front sides of the sweater slant downward from the neck before meeting somewhere on the chest or below, where they are fastened by the top button.

THE COLLAR NECK. In this nonspecific style, the neckline, whatever it happens to be

THE CREW NECK. The name comes from the style of sweater worn by English collegiate boat crews. The round neckline hugs the throat with a half- to a full-inch band of ribbing that's different from the knitted body portion.

THE HENLEY NECK. Another rounded neck, what distinguishes this style is that the neck of the sweater is split in front by a two- or more-buttoned flap.

THE MOCK TURTLENECK. Actually, this style is closer to the crew neck than the turtleneck, since the neckband is usually ribbed in an exaggerated neck width so the neck of the sweater rises slightly above the collar line but is not folded down.

THE RING NECK. Another crew variation, this is sometimes called a *French crew neck*. The round neckband is thin, probably not ribbed, but instead finished with a knitted edge.

THE SHAWL NECK. Usually called the shawl collar, the style has an attached, rolled-back collar of a curving, elongated outline without indentations.

THE TURTLENECK. This familiar neckline has a tubular, high turned-over collar that folds as many as three times while hugging the throat.

THE V-NECK. A self-describing style, the neckline forms a V. Classically collarless, contemporary sweaters often break with tradition, so it's not unusual to discover a V-neck sweater with a ribbed, rolled-back collar or some other collar variation.

SHOULDERS

THE DOLMAN SHOULDER. This is a stylized look of very deeply drooping armholes, with the long sleeves snug at the wrists. When the droop is the droopiest, the style is called *batwing,* for obvious reasons.

THE DROPPED SHOULDER. Not especially widely seen in menswear, this shoulder interpretation extends the shoulder line far wider than normal, so the shoulder seam falls on the upper arm, hence the description of dropped.

THE RAGLAN SHOULDER. The sleeves of the sweater extend to the neckline with slanting seamlines from under the armholes up to the collar line in front and back, producing a relatively undefined shoulder area. The style is named for General Lord Raglan, who came up with the design for his soldiers during the Crimean War.

THE SET-IN SHOULDER. As with suits and shirts, set-in shoulders have sleeves cut separately from the garment's body and seamed at the armholes. This is the most typical shoulder style.

THE SPLIT SHOULDER. This combination of raglan and set-in shoulders can have a set-in front and raglan back or vice versa.

KNITS

Knitting techniques are endless, but what really counts is the end result on the body. The knits that make the most difference in affecting body proportions follow.

BASKET WEAVE. While the name specifies a weave as opposed to a knit, the identifiable look can be, and often is, knitted, producing boxes of knitted areas (small or large) to give an overall raised/dropped effect resembling a plaited basket.

BOUCLÉ. Bouclés have bumpy surfaces that appear looped or knotted; from the French word for curled or, strictly, buckled.

CABLE KNIT. This stitch, which is often used in conjunction with other stitches, yields a heavy

cord made up of raised, looped, overlapping stripes that together resemble a cable.

FLAT KNIT. The name says it all.

PLAIN KNIT. Plainly, the simplest knit, when each loop is held by the one above.

POPCORN. Another aptly named appearance, it is a bouclé gone wild.

RIB KNIT. This produces, naturally, a ribbed effect. One well-known example is the *shaker sweater* with its heavy yarns knitted in a plain ribbed stitch.

ALL ABOUT OUTERWEAR

As the term conveys, outerwear is worn out of doors as the outer layer of clothing—usually. An *overcoat* is a warm coat, heavier presumably than a *topcoat,* but both are outer garments made of fabric or fur. *Car coats* refer more to a length and a look than to weight or warmth. *Jackets* tend to be shorter than coats but can't be dress jackets in the way that dress coats may be so described, even though some jackets can adopt a dressy attitude. With all these and those hairline distinctions, how does one begin understanding outerwear? By plunging in.

THE DRESS COAT

Once these words described the type of coat conventionally required for full-dress formal occasions. No more. Now dress coats are those worn with business suits or even sport jackets. Given the different modes of male attire, some dress coats are dressier than others. If the coat isn't long enough to at least graze the knees, it most often won't win the dress description.

THE BALMACAAN. This familiar style with the unfamiliar name is a rather countrified dress coat that's loose and full. Named after an estate near Inverness in Scotland, the balmacaan has raglan sleeves and is usually made of a rough woolen fabric. Its most characteristic touch is the moderately narrow *bal collar* (a shortening of the entire name), similar to and often interchangable with the *convertible collar.* It can be worn unbuttoned and flat, so it looks like a large-sized, open-at-the-neck shirt collar; or, the top button can be fastened, and then the collar looks even more like a bigger version of a buttoned-to-the-top shirt collar worn without a tie. The collar can also be turned up all around, buttoned or not.

THE CHESTERFIELD. This topcoat began its fashion life as a single-breasted, fly-front overcoat with a plain, center-vented back and a slightly shaped waist. The notched lapel was joined to a velvet collar, as worn in the 18th century by the fourth earl of Chesterfield. Today it's more often, though far from necessarily, double-breasted, but the velvet collar survives in various interpretations of the look. The chesterfield is one of the dressier dress coats.

THE FUR COAT. Covering a range of lengths, a fur coat can be in nearly any style so long as it's made of fur, whatever the origins. The same is true of suede and leather coats. Styling determines whether they are dressy or casual.

THE GREATCOAT. With this self-effacing name, the greatcoat was initially fur-lined but now

refers to any coat cut with generous, perhaps overly-generous, proportions, often in very heavy fabrics.

THE POLO COAT. It was popularized by polo players in the 1920s when it was a double-breasted outercoat, rather loosely fitting with a full belt or a half-belt across the back, in camel's hair. It had large flapped patch pockets and was often made with raglan sleeves. The basic ingredients remain in today's version, but the coat may be single-breasted, may have set-in sleeves, and probably is made of a blend or an imitation of camel's hair. In fact, the contemporary polo coat comes in many colors.

THE REEFER COAT. The coat, as opposed to the reefer jacket, is difficult to pinpoint since it's a coat-coat without any dramatically differentiating features. It tends to be somewhat fitted and tailored, with buttons exposed instead of hidden by a fly front, and comes in a sturdy fabric. Single- or double-breasted, it's what you probably think of when you hear the word topcoat.

THE TRENCH COAT. Some might argue that this old standby should not be considered a dress coat. In practice, of course, it's one of the most pervasive coat styles worn with suits, as rainwear or not. The name is derived from the fact that a similar topcoat style was worn by British officers in the trenches during World War I, later by United States officers in World War II. The original model

was double-breasted, had reinforced shoulder flaps and gun flaps, a multitude of pockets, and was belted.

Sticklers will also say that a trench coat isn't a trench coat if it's single-breasted and lacks epaulets (shoulders tabs or ornaments that button or buckle and which, surprisingly, weren't always on the originals). Well, let the sticklers vocalize, but no one listens to their swan songs any more.

The trench coat has become a generic style. Vaguely military-influenced coats are called *military coats.* Rainwear is often in the military or trench feel and can be either *waterproofed* (meaning the raincoats are coated with a substance to close the pores of the fabric) or *water-*

repellent (a finishing process causing water to shed from the surface—up to a point; in a deluge, a water-repellent coat can become waterlogged).

THE WRAP COAT. It does what it says, wraps, by overlapping in front without any buttons. It is secured in place with a belt that usually ties but may buckle.

PERIOD COATS. Most often these are faddish interpretations of styles worn during one historical period or another. *Regency* and *Edwardian coats,* for example, are two styles named after specific eras. In general, period coats usually have very nipped-in waists and flaring skirts with deep vents.

THE CASUAL COAT

It would be nice to say that all casual coats hover above the knees. Nice, but incorrect. Take a straight-hanging coat that reaches mid-calf. Picture it in a horseblanket plaid or rainbow stripes. A dress coat it isn't.

Or take what has come to be known as the *British warm*. It was a heavy, warm overcoat favored by British army officers during World War I. Today, it's a classic style—double-breasted, subtly-shaped, often but not necessarily with two sharply slanting patch pockets and with epaulets at the shoulders. Originally taupe-colored, many-colored British warms have to today's eye a tailored, dressy aspect, certainly more so than many box dress coats. Even so, since most come in above-the-knee lengths, British warms are classified as casual coats. This omission hasn't stopped loads of men from wearing them as dress coats.

THE CAR COAT. It comes in a variety of styles in any fabric imaginable. Supposedly a more comfortable cut for driving, a car coat hovers in lengths from the hip to mid-thigh. In a hip-length, some might call the garment a jacket.

THE DUFFEL COAT. Its name can be traced to Duffel, Belgium, where the heavy wool fabric typical of duffel coats was originally woven. Hooded, although sometimes the hood is detachable, the classic model has toggle closures of wood or horn, is loose-fitting and stops mid-to-lower thigh. Some interpretations reach the knee and beyond. The style is sometimes called a *toggle coat.*

THE HUDSON BAY COAT. This hefty, thigh-touching coat is usually double-breasted in white or off-white with two or three colorful stripes encircling the lower portion. Similar in outdoorsy appeal are *blanket coats,* which look as if they are made from thick plain blanketing material, and *mackinaws,* belted blanket variations of heavy plaid wool, named after Mackinac, Michigan, a

distribution center in colonial days where blankets and clothes were given to the Indians.

LODEN COATS. Loden refers to both a specific fabric and a general style. The coating fabric is fleecy, made from greasy, naturally water-repellent wool, usually in a distinctive green color, also known as loden. The style is double-breasted with a yoked front and back, and has wooden toggle or button closures. (A *yoke* is a fitted portion of a garment, usually—and in this case—over the shoulders, to which the body of the garment is seamed and sewn.)

MELTON COATS. Melton isn't a style at all, only a fabric description. The typical melton fabric is thick and heavy, finished so the nap is somewhat fuzzy.

RANCH COATS. These look at home on the range. Often shearling-lined, they generate a feeling of the Old West and usually don't extend below the knee, often stopping at the hip. The style has, however, been adapted into a semidress, longer version. Often in suede or pigskin, ranch coats can come in utilitarian woven fabrics such as corduroy and denim.

THE SWEATER COAT. An amply proportioned garment that, given its name, quite reasonably represents an extension of sweater styling into outerwear. The sweater coat is usually knitted but comes in woven versions. Considering the lattitude in sweaters, this coat category, which bounded into prominence in the late 70s, is limitless in expression.

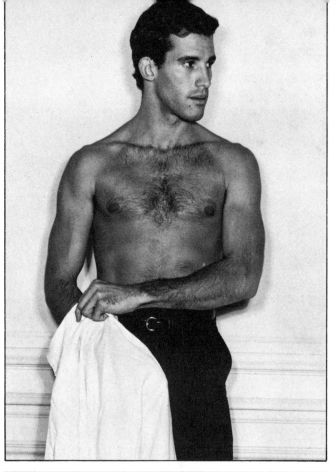

A three-piece suit

splits for new companions.

A V-neck sweater does double-time.

A classic blazer can scorn tradition.

Dressing down never hurts.

ALL ABOUT SWIMWEAR

Men have no shame.

That would be the outcry of turn-of-the-century Victorians if they could see what passes muster—and legality—for bathing attire today. In some secluded corners, the only appropriate beachwear is the bare ass.

In brief, the swimwear story centers on how much a man wants to cover up or, conversely, how much baring his body can bear without catalyzing waves of protest from offended sensibilities. Only the best bodies can flaunt them.

THE TRUNKS

THE BIKINI. There's not much to say. Next to the *monokini,* hardly more than a supporting pouch on a string (more publicized than worn), the bikini is the briefest swimsuit around. It may be two inches wide at the sides, even less, but decency prescribes that coverage from the crotch to the low-slung waist keep pubic hair under wrap.

THE BRIEF. Also a style of underwear, the brief style in swimwear covers nearly the same area as brief underwear, with the same fluctuations. In other words, some briefs are briefer than others, although all are close-fitting. Flyless, slim *racers* are one brief variety. Most briefs, in fact, are flyless, although some have nonfunctional fly details. Briefs are usually cut close enough so that supporters are unnecessary, although some are

double layered with a same-sized or smaller inner-lining that passes for support but is really there as a nod toward modesty.

BOXERS. Influenced by the sport, boxers can be very amply cut or in trimmer proportions. Common to all is a puckered waist, in most instances an elasticized one, although some boxers have drawstring waists. The legs tend to be baggy, so either a jockstrap or a fabric shell

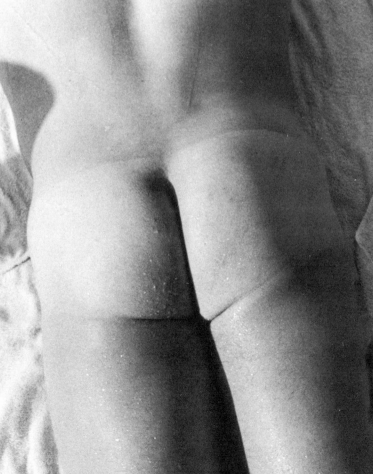

serving in the same capacity is pretty much a necessity.

JAMS. These are long-legged (to about the knee) models of swimwear associated with surfing. A drawstring waist is about the only universal feature.

SHORTS. Various items masquerade as swimwear. In dire straits, a business suit could be a bathing suit. When the mood strikes but the real thing isn't available, walking shorts, cut-off jeans or any abbreviated shorts become swimwear too.

THE WET SUIT. Skin-fitting rubberized garments used for protection, they are, or should be, purely functional and aren't given to making fashion statements. When worn to that end, they are an affectation.

THE TOPS

Except for true tank tops, those of the same rubberized material and worn with wet suit bottoms, swim tops aren't for swimming these days. What is commonly called a *tank top* is a sleeveless shirt in an underwear style, although often in various colors and fabrics. It may or may not be sold as a companion to swim trunks. *Cabana sets,* with shirt-styled tops matching the trunks, seem fairly much anachronisms. Today swimwear tops often pick up other motifs— jogging-type jackets, for example—and are only loosely coordinated, if at all, with bathing suits.

BEACHWEAR

This is clothing worn to, fro or on the beach. It can be about anything as long as it strips down easily. A beachwear ensemble might consist of sandals, drawstring pants (over the trunks), a bare chest and a towel draped over the shoulders. Or it can be a whole decked-out outfit. In most instances, except by the extreme fashion savages, beachwear isn't specially sought out and consists of a sport shirt over casual pants or shorts. At posh resorts, maybe some people still give a damn. At public beaches, anything goes and usually does.

ALL ABOUT SHOES

It's often said that a man's shoe wardrobe is every bit as important as his clothing selection.

Footwear can be categorized as dress, casual, sport and work. Boots squeeze in relative to use. More important than style is fit, however. Abe Lincoln said he couldn't think when his feet hurt, and that's a universal condition.

DRESS SHOES

Needless to say, one man's dress shoe isn't another's. Lace-ups are considered dressier than slip-ons, but exceptions abound. The dressiest shoe around is the formal patent leather pump, a slip-on. Combat boots are lace-ups but hardly dress shoes. Penny loafers, though widely worn with suits, are thought of as casual shoes, but tassled loafers are dressier than lace-up saddle shoes.

Here are some fairly common styles that usually pass inspection as dress shoes.

BROGUES. This is a generic term for heavy, strong shoes trimmed with perforations and stitchings. The *wingtip* is one example. Perforated toe designs are called medallions.

CAP TOES. These shoes have an additional outer covering at the tip of the shoe, usually applied straight across. This "cap" may or may not be perforated.

CORDOVANS. Actually, cordovan is a leather made from the inner hide of a horse's rump and tanned with vegetable materials to reach both its characteristic color and its nonporous state. The strong, highly buffed leather has a dressy appearance in either lace-ups or slip-ons, although it's used in casual shoes too.

GILLIES. These laced shoes have no tongues. They are a variation of oxfords.

KILTIES. Sometimes called shawl tongues, these shoes have a leather fringe (sometimes removable) that's draped over the instep of the shoe, covering the laces and eyelets. Like gillies, they are often considered only casual shoes.

LOAFERS. Depending upon details, some slip-ons are thought of as dress shoes, those with perforated medallions in particular. Thin-soled,

soft-leathered loafers are sometimes acceptable, sometimes not.

MONK-STRAPS. These are usually plain-toed shoes with a strap and buckle to fasten across the instep.

OXFORDS. The most familiar style among lace-ups, they are fairly low-cut shoes often ending at the instep with three or more eyelets, laced and tied. Usually the toes are plain and rounded. Oxfords come in a variety of leathers and textures but are generally more lightweight than brogues, which often have more eyelets.

SEAMLESS TOES. As the name states, these shoes have no seams on the toe area. In fact, the upper (nonsole) portion of the shoe is all one piece, stitched only in the back.

CASUAL SHOES

Obviously, some dress shoes do double duty as casual footwear, as do some sport shoes as well. Moccasin-inspired shoes (such as heelless topsiders) are definitely casual, as opposed to dress, shoes. Espadrilles—those canvas, rope-soled knockabouts—and sneakers (originally worn for tennis) get the casual tag but are often worn with blazers at resorts. Sandals aren't actually shoes, but they are casual.

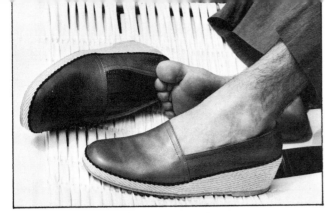

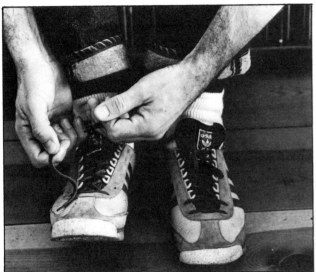

SPORT SHOES

They are different from casual shoes only in that they were designed for active sports. Some, like baseball and golf shoes, are cleated and are hazards as street wear. Others, such as jogging and tennis shoes, prove that active sport outfittings often cross the line into casual clothing in general.

WORK SHOES

These styles often hit the streets as casual wearables. By definition, though, work shoes are any style of shoe or boot designed for sturdiness, comfort and protection of the foot, often having hefty soles, weather-proofed linings or other reinforcements.

BOOTS

Cowboy boots are the most ubiquitous style, but boots come in endless variety. With their higher heels, boots will change trouser length proportions. Someone who wears boots often may need two pants wardrobes: one for flat-heeled footwear, another for boots. *Chukka* (boots extending above the ankle and fastened with a lace through two eyelets) and *bush* (also called desert) styles have lower heels than those found on cowboys but can nonetheless distort trousers' length dimensions.

ALL ABOUT FABRICS

The principles of weaving are elemental—two threads (or yarns) meet at perpendicular angles, then one goes over, one goes under, the other. From this simple joining, many variations and complexities arise. Lengthwise threads or yarns are called the *warp*. Those going over and under as *filling* horizontally are called the *weft*.

Three basic weaves exist, from which many fabric effects emerge in seemingly infinite variety.

THE PLAIN WEAVE

It is the simplest. Each filling or weft yarn goes over, then under, then over and under again, each warp yarn successively to form an even surface. Rows alternate, so the next weft goes under the warp that the preceding weft went over, and so forth.

When the system of interlacing incorporates either heavier warp or weft yarns than used in the other direction, or if yarns in either are further apart in one direction than those in the other direction, then a regularly ribbed surface is produced. This is called a *rib weave*. Nonetheless, the rib weave is classified as a plain weave, since the filling threads continue passing over and under the warp threads in alternating rows. The *basket weave,* which yields an open, rough fabric by passing pairs of warp over pairs of filling yarns, is another variation.

THE TWILL WEAVE

This basic weave is identifiable by a distinct diagonal line or rib, either left or right. As the fabric is being woven, the filling yarn goes over two or more warp yarns, but under one or more warp yarns. Repeated progressively, this type of bypassing creates the diagonal effect.

When this method of interlacing is redirected, then changed back again repeatedly, to form continuous patterns of V's, the result is a zigzag, chevron effect called *herringbone,* because of the supposed resemblance to the fish's skeleton. This variation of the twill weave is often described as the *broken twill weave.*

THE SATIN WEAVE

Sometimes called a broken twill weave, it is more often considered a true third basic weave. The weft yarns pass over several warp yarns before going under a smaller number of the weft, then once again pass several more warp yarns

before going under a smaller number again. This technique produces a smooth, lustrous surface, because the floating surface yarns catch more light. The fabric named satin is the shining example of the weave.

In addition to the three basic weaves, there are mechanical devices which produce characteristic fabrics but which are referred to as weaves. The *Jacquard weave* actually is named for the Jacquard attachment that allows a loom to produce very intricate patterns, small or large, during the weaving process. Ditto for the *dobby weave.* A dobby is another special loom attachment, this time to produce smaller patterns. The attachment is not as complicated as the Jacquard, nor are the resulting designs as intricate.

How a fabric is woven (or knitted) will affect its character. Of course, so will the fiber employed, whether natural or synthetic, and how the yarns are produced. *Worsted fabrics,* for example, are made of worsted yarns—firm, strong, smooth-surfaced yarns spun from combed wool—as opposed to *woolen* yarns, which are fuzzier and softer because the wool is not combed prior to being spun into yarn.

These subtleties and technicalities, however, are better left to fabric stylists. As had been said before, how garments help a man dress right is what really matters; how the garments come to look a certain way is often incidental.

But since fabric weaves can visually affect some somatotypes, a quick glimpse at some fabrics commonly used is in order. These same fabrics may be used in suits, sport coats, pants, some outerwear, perhaps certain shirts, maybe even a tie or two or several.

CAVALRY TWILL. A very stout twill weave—considered to be one of the hardier fabrics—cavalry twill fabrics have very definite diagonal cords. (A *corded fabric* has a raised rib effect.)

CHINO. Initially a twilled cotton fabric used for military uniforms, today the name chino is applied to any medium-weight but sturdy fabric that has a slight sheen. Military tan and khaki green shades with some luster are among the most common colors for chino pants, but they come in others.

CHEVIOT. A twill-woven woolen or worsted fabric, cheviots are rough-surfaced and often

napped (having a somewhat fuzzy appearance). Similar to serge the typical cheviot is heavier and rougher. Originally cheviot fabrics were made from the coarse, shaggy wool of the sheep of the Cheviot Hills on the border between England and Scotland.

CORDUROY. Either a plain- or twill-weave fabric, traditionally made of cotton, this material has woven or sheared ribs on a smooth, often velvet-like surface. Very narrow ribs are called *pin wales;* more separated furrows and ridges are *wide wales*. In medieval times, the fabric was worn by members of the king's outdoor service, hence the name corduroy from *corde du roi,* which literally translates as threads of the king.

DENIM. Another name derived from the French, *de Nîmes* (from Nîmes), where it may have originated, denim is also another firm twill fabric. Officially it has colored warp threads and white filling which impart a powdery effect. But when the fabric's look became the rage in jeans, denim joined the common vocabulary as meaning any fabric that looked vaguely like the original. Its surface can be brushed, to create a downlike nap.

FLANNEL. A soft, light fabric, usually with a brushed surface and loosely woven in either a plain or twill weave. Traditionally, flannel is made of cotton or wool, although flannel may be in just about any fiber. The fabric is napped only on the exterior side. It is made in varying weights, so flannel trousers can be heavier than flannel shirts.

Flannel comes from the Welsh *gwlanen,* which means added to wool.

GABARDINE. This time the origins are Spanish, from *gabardina,* once meaning a woolen cloak. Naturally, today's gabardine fabrics aren't necessarily made of wool. Gabardine is a medium to heavyweight twilled and worsted material. Being a twill weave, it has the fine diagonal rib effect. The surface can be hard and smooth or soft and dull, in solid or iridescent colors.

HERRINGBONE. This broken twill weave creates a series of V patterns. While a fabric, it can be considered a texture or a pattern.

HOPSACKING. This is another of those strange ones. The word is still bandied about with less than specific denotation. Once used to describe a type of burlap bagging, now hopsacking might better be called a basket weave and not a fabric, but saying so won't stop people from doing it.

KHAKI. Derived from the Hindu word meaning dust-colored, khaki was originally a brownish-greenish twill cotton fabric used for uniforms in the Anglo-Indian army. Now khaki refers both to the olive-drab color and to fabrics made in these colors, be the fibers wool, cotton or manmade.

MADRAS. A firm, hand-loomed cotton fabric imported from Madras, India, woven in satin, basket or figured weaves, often in colorful plaids, checks or stripes, sometimes intermingled. True madras fabrics invariably bleed when laundered, fading considerably and staining other garments in the same wash.

POPLIN. A fine, durable, light to medium-weight material, usually of cotton, poplin is made to look somewhat like silk with a fine horizontal rib created by a plain weave with the warp threads finer than the filling threads.

SAXONY. Originating in Saxony, Germany, saxony refers both to a closely twisted, fine yarn and to napped fabrics made from the fine wool of sheep raised in the region. The fabric can be lightweight flannel, fine cheviot, or tweed, in solid colors or chalk stripes.

SEERSUCKER. A thin, lightweight fabric with crinkling, alternating stripes is the characteristic seersucker appearance. This effect is achieved during the plain-weaving process by varying the tensions in the warp (vertical) yarns, so that the looser yarns pucker when the firmer filling yarns are woven in.

SERGE. A smooth-surfaced material woven in an even twill with worsted yarns, serge fabrics exhibit the characteristic diagonals on both sides. Traditionally made of wool, serge today comes in many fibers and blends.

SHARKSKIN. This smooth-surfaced fabric usually has a distinctive luster, since it is made in a twill weave utilizing two tones of yarns.

TWEED. Tweed fabrics may be produced in plain, twill or herringbone weaves. Formerly all-wool *homespun* (coarse-surfaced, once hand-made) materials produced first in Scotland by crofters on the Tweed River, today tweeds are characteristically rather rough, rugged, often nubby fabrics. Some have *slubs,* unevenly textured areas with thick nubs in the yarn, sometimes imperfections or else purposefully engineered. *Harris tweed* is a registered trademark for material woven on the islands of the Outer Hebrides off the west coast of Scotland (Harris is one of the islands). This tweed is very soft and usually hand-woven in a variety of checks and plaids. *Donegal tweed* was first made by hand in County Donegal, Ireland. Today the term is applied to nearly any tweed material that has thick, most often colored, slubs.

VELVET. The well-known fabric with thick, short, closely-woven pile, velvet is produced by

various methods, one more complicated than the other. *Velour* and *velveteen* are less expensive versions. *Uncut velvet* has a looped surface rather than the standard plushness.

WHIPCORD is an extremely strong, diagonal twill-woven worsted fabric that resembles gabardine but that is much heavier. This fabric comes with emphatic round cords, narrow or wide. Due to this great durability, whipcords are often used in uniforms and riding clothes.

ALL ABOUT PATTERNS

In recent years, we've come a long way in men's clothing. Although clothes have calmed down since the dizzying flights during the so-called Peacock Revolution in the 1960s, the patterns employed in menswear today aren't nearly as somber and sober as they were during the conservative 50s.

Few patterns are exclusively designated as either masculine or feminine, although certain ones appear more frequently in menswear than others. Stripes, checks and plaids are found on any item of male apparel, whereas florals and fantasies are more often confined to ties and sportswear.

Here are the major pattern families commonly associated with men's clothing.

STRIPES

Everyone knows what a stripe looks like—simply a band of color atop an expanse of another color. Usually used in multiples, stripes contrast with the background of the fabric, called the *ground,* so that the stripes are more prominent when the contrast is greater. Stripes can be very narrow or very broad, and terminology defining them usually but not always refers to the width.

HAIRLINE STRIPES. These are the thinnest of stripes, often of white, sometimes in a color. They are usually, but not necessarily, spaced evenly from each other.

PIN STRIPES. These very slender stripes can be in any color, though often they're gray or white on a darker ground. They can be as narrow as a pin, never wider than one-sixteenth of an inch. Pin stripes can be narrowly or widely spaced, although the distance between them should remain constant.

PENCIL STRIPES. Next in scale up from pin stripes, these are about the width of a mark made with a dull pencil. They can be any distance from the next stripe in the series.

CHALK STRIPES. So named because they appear to be drawn with a piece of chalk, they are obviously wider than pencil stripes and are usually white; chalk stripes are consistent in their spacing from each other.

REGIMENTAL STRIPES. Associated with neckwear, they come in even diagonal stripes that were originally in the colors of a particular British regiment but are now mainly suggestive of those distinctive stripings. Some are still authentic.

SATIN STRIPES. These are associated with shirting fabrics, where a stripe of a satin weave is woven into a fabric of another basic weave, so the satin stripes appear more lustrous even when they are the same color as the ground.

SHADOW STRIPES. They're not really stripes in the usual sense but give an indistinct striped impression due to the type of weave, achieved by alternating warp yarns of the same color but of different tightness. The term shadow is applied because the striped effect is produced by light hitting the yarns differently.

CHECKS

A check pattern is composed of contrasting squares of any size (although they are often relatively small) which are repeated to resemble, with some variations, a checkerboard. The name check also applies to each individual square.

BROKEN CHECKS. Although the placing of the individual checks remains regular, the design of each square or check is irregular, that is, does not form a perfect square. Each imperfect square is uniform in its irregularity. A popular example is the houndstooth, large or small, vividly or subtly contrasting, each irregular square simulating a canine tooth and repeated regularly.

BUFFALO CHECKS. These are sometimes called a plaid, but plaids need not be based on squares. Buffalo checks are big squares in blocks of color, usually red and black, generally on heavy fabrics. Some so-called lumberjack plaids are buffalo checks.

GLEN CHECKS. These are district checks, each one unique to a particular glen (in Scottish, originally meaning valley) or area. The patterns usually consist of varying colored checks which have other checks or lines in different colors imposed over them. Frequently used in tweeds, glen checks cover a broad range of colors and are often also referred to as glen plaids.

GUN CLUB CHECKS. Also widely used in tweeds, these are double checked designs consisting of a big check superimposed over a small one.

OVERCHECKS. The term covers both glen and gun club checks. Generically overchecks may have two or more checks, one over the other.

PIN CHECKS. A checked pattern in which the squares are extremely small, smaller than a shepherd check.

SHEPHERD CHECKS. Designs of small, even checks in black and white, brown and white, or occasionally other contrasting colors. One theory for the name's origin is that the wool for it could be shorn from the sheep and woven without any dyeing. Many shepherd checks are also district checks.

TATTERSALL CHECKS. They are regularly-spaced overchecks framed by horizontal and vertical stripes generally in two colors on a light-colored ground, similar to the checks on some English horse blankets once used by Richard Tattersall. An example is blue stripes running horizontally, brown ones running vertically, on a tan ground. According to traditional shirting specifications, the lines should cross at less than one-inch intervals and are frequently much closer together than that, though seldom wider.

PLAIDS

These wide-ranging patterns are composed of bars of varied, multiple stripes which cross each other at right angles to form squares or rectangles of different designs and/or colors that are regularly repeated.

ARGYLE PLAID. Like the design of argyle socks, this plaid is made of small but more often

GLEN PLAID. A shortening of Glenurquhart plaid, characteristically this design consists of squares of small woven checks alternating with same-sized squares of larger checks, often utilizing one or two colors with white. However, while the foregoing describes the classic Glenurquhart, plaids of greatly divergent appearances are commonly called glen plaids, probably because the Scots produced such a wealth of district checks and plaids.

HUNTING PLAID. Likewise originating in Scotland, the hunting plaid is another generic type. Many versions were worn by different clans while hunting or for everyday dress. The colors often harmonized with the landscape, so the hunters could surreptitiously blend into the surroundings while pursuing their quarry.

LATTICE PLAID. A simple plaid pattern woven in squares separated by narrow bands to set off the squares.

OVERPLAID. As the name implies, two or more plaids are combined together to appear as if one is atop the other.

large diamonds, usually with contrasting diagonal thin overstripes running through the diamonds, creating other diamond designs.

BLANKET PLAID. This plaid is quite large and often comes in dark but rich colors with lighter-colored overstriping.

TARTAN PLAID. Once again, this is a generic description covering any of many distinctively designed plaids (tartans) of various Scotch Highland clans.

WINDOWPANE PLAID. In contrast to the sometimes intricate tartan plaids, this simple motif has stripes (either singly or doubly) running both vertically and horizontally to produce a large barred framework of rectangles said to resemble windowpanes.

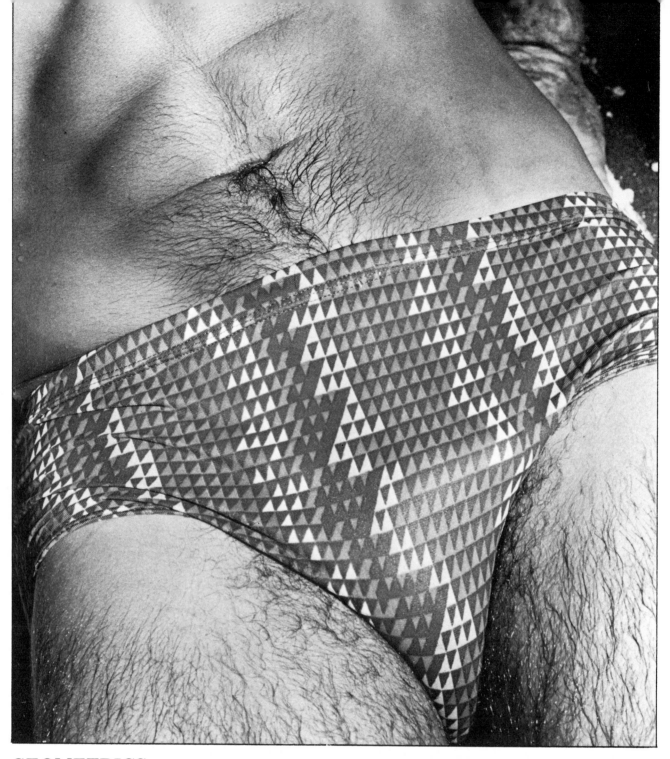

GEOMETRICS

Geometric patterns are just that, designs based on geometric figures, such as circles, squares, triangles, hexagons. The shapes may be used alone or in various combinations, vastly scaled or undersized.

Certain designs are offshoots of geometric patterns, often due to the type of weave employed. The *birdseye* design, for example, has small, somewhat triangular shapes overall, with small, centered dots resembling (some say) a bird's eye. *Structured patterns* became very important in suitings in the late 70s. Often in tweeds, the fabrics then and still are not distinctly geometric but only vaguely suggest tiny geometric shapes because of variations of texture.

Paisley might fancifully be considered a fluid interpretation of the triangle, softening and curving the three sides. Or the characteristic design might be said to look like an amoeba convention. Whether or not it's considered a geometric or a fantasy print, paisley is used widely in menswear in neckwear and, from time to time, other items too.

DOTS

When they're big enough, dots could conceivably be considered geometric patterns too, but since they run their own dotty distances, they deserve a separate but short listing. They are usually positioned in a regular pattern, although they can appear randomly. Sizes mainly determine how they are named.

Polka dots are probably the most well-known. They are about the size of an average aspirin and not the more petite ones that are often mistakenly called polka dots. Their other name, *aspirin dots,* is more descriptive.

Coin dots are even larger, from the size of a nickel up to that of a quarter. Higher change would be approaching circles, no longer dots. It's a toss-up whether to call dots dimensioned like dimes polka or coin dots. *Pin dots,* on the other hand, are among the smallest dots used and may be no larger than the head of a pin. *Confetti dots* are bigger than pin dots, in fact can be of about any size. Unlike the earlier versions, which are usually in one or occasionally two colors, confetti dots are many-colored and are more likely to be spaced randomly.

FLORALS, FIGURES, FANTASIES

These three *F*'s pretty much round out the list of patterns used in menswear.

FLORALS. They come in all varieties, from tidy little buds neatly arranged to the foliage found on Hawaiian shirts blooming in vivid profusion. Generally relegated to ties and sport shirts, florals from time to time enjoy brief spurts of importance on dress shirtings.

FIGURES. These pictorialize human or non-human living creatures in some type of design motif, more often appearing on sweaters than other garments. In the early to mid-70s, a flurry of "conversational" prints were introduced in shirts. These either suggested dramatic scenes or actually incorporated cartoonlike dialogue. The craze was short-lived.

FANTASIES. They are the stuff that dreamy or nightmarish fabrics are made of. They fit no other category, being the fanciest of all patterns, sometimes incorporating florals and figures or paisleys in any conceivable colorations.

CONTRAPUNTAL PATTERNS

These may incorporate a bit of the fantastic or not, mainly not. Essentially, they are a combination of two or more pattern motifs in a single pattern, such as taking a basic argyle and placing florals within the regular sets of the diamonds, or breaking up conventional plaids with periodic bold bands of contrasting stripes. Although some of the combinations can sound gruesome, they need not be if attention is paid to scale and colorations.

POSTSCRIPT

When all is said and done—and this is it for *Dressing Right*—clothes are what you do with them, how you see them. Even after reading these exhortations to get into the spirit of clothes, some fellows will still want dictates and never-to-be-broken rules. I can't give them, and won't, simply because clothing commandments are wrong. The guidelines I've assembled reflect *my* view of so-called men's fashion. *Yours* needn't be mine. Hopefully, reading about clothes in this new way has helped you see clothing in a new, more enjoyable perspective. You should have fun dressing yourself.

I'm constantly surprised when I pick up an issue of *L'Uomo Vogue*, the Italian men's fashion magazine, or even when I'm strolling along the street, to see how someone has put together a terrific look. I ask myself, "Why didn't I think of that?" Then, tempering my vanity with as much modesty as I can muster, I mentally respond, "Hix, you don't know it all. No one does." Sorry, I don't have all the answers. And I'm glad that I don't, because surprises are always awaiting me.

Surprise yourself. Take a giant leap into dressing right, your way, not mine or anyone else's. Good energy goes on generating itself. Charge.

ACKNOWLEDGMENTS

Austin Reed of Regent Street
Jeffrey Banks
Jhane Barnes
Stanley Blacker
Bill Blass
Brooks Bros. (New York)
Camouflage (New York)
Pierre Cardin
Ilona Cardona
Catalina
Sal Cesarani
Charles Gallay (Beverly Hills)
Ron Chereskin
Joe Collins
Country Britches
Vicky Davis
Oscar de La Renta
Alan Flusser for
  Pierre Cardin Relax
Gleneagles
The Good Old Days (New York)
Graham & Gunn, Ltd.
T.T. Gurtner
Hart Schaffner & Marx
Hickey-Freeman

I. Buss & Co. (New York)
Interqueros
Jantzen
Alexander Julian
Bill Kaiserman for Rafael
Kerr Sport Shop (Beverly Hills)
Nancy Knox Ltd.
Ronald Kolodzie
Glen Patrick Magary
Makins Hats
Maxfield Bleu (Beverly Hills)
Men's Fashion Association
Calvin Klein
Petkanas Bros.
Bert Pulitzer
Yves St. Laurent
Brian Scott-Carr
David Shapiro for Ursel
Robert Stock for Country Roads
Charles Suppon
Gil Truedsson for Tiger of Sweden
Joan Vass
Egon Von Furstenberg
Lee Wright for G.B. Pedrini
  & San Remo

COVER Clothes by Alexander Julian
P. 13 *Left*, shirt by Sal Cesarani
P. 25 *Lower left*, clothes by Gil Truedsson for Tiger of Sweden
P. 28 *Top*, styled by Robert Stock; *bottom*, clothes by Alan Flusser for Pierre
Cardin Relax
P. 32 Clothes by Lee Wright for G.B. Pedrini
P. 33 Clothes by Alexander Julian
P. 37 Clothes by Alan Flusser for Pierre Cardin Relax
P. 38 Clothes by Alexander Julian
P. 40 Vest by David Shapiro for Ursel
P. 44 Clothes by Gil Truedsson for Tiger of Sweden
P. 46 Suit by Jeffrey Banks
P. 47 Clothes from Charles Gallay (Beverly Hills)
P. 48-49 Clothes by Lee Wright for G.B. Pedrini & San Remo

P. 55 *Left*, T-shirt by Ronald Kolodzie
P. 59 *Top*, sweaters by Joan Vass; *lower left*, shirt by Bill Kaiserman for Rafael, pants by Alexander Julian
P. 60 *Lower left*, shirt by Glen Patrick Magary, vest by Joe Collins; *lower right*, shirt/vest by Ron Chereskin
P. 64 Clothes by Alexander Julian
P. 66 *Bottom*, clothes by Lee Wright for G.B. Pedrini
P. 68 Sport jacket from Graham & Gunn, Ltd., shirt & tie by Bert Pulitzer
P. 71 Suit & sweater by Gil Truedsson for Tiger of Sweden
P. 72 *Lower right*, shirt & tie by Charles Suppon
P. 74 *Lower left*, jacket by Charles Suppon; *top right*, clothes from I. Buss & Co. (New York)
P. 79 Clothes by Jhane Barnes
P. 80 Jacket by Stanley Blacker
P. 81 *Left*, jacket by Charles Suppon; *right*, jacket by Brian Scott-Carr, vest by Joe Collins
P. 84 *Left*, clothes by Bill Blass; *right*, suit jacket by Austin Reed of Regent Street, sweater by Bert Pulitzer
P. 87 Jacket from Brooks Bros., shirt by Bert Pulitzer
P. 88-91 Clothes styled by designer Sal Cesarani; shoes by Interqueros; coat by Lee Wright for San Remo
P. 92-93 Suit by Austin Reed of Regent Street, shirt by Bert Pulitzer, coat by Gleneagles
P. 94-97 Coat & suit by Pierre Cardin
P. 98 Clothes by Alexander Julian
P. 99 Clothes styled by Alan Flusser
P. 100-101 Clothes from Charles Gallay (Beverly Hills)
P. 102 Clothes by Jhane Barnes
P. 105 T-shirt & jacket by Ronald Kolodzie
P. 107 *Lower right*, sweater by Robert Stock for Country Roads, sandals from Maxfield Bleu (Beverly Hills)
P. 108 Sportswear by Jantzen
P. 110 Outfits by Ron Chereskin (*left*), Catalina (*right*)
P. 112 Jacket by Jhane Barnes, pants by Ilona Cardona
P. 113 Sweater, shirt & tie by Bert Pulitzer
P. 117 Clothes from Kerr Sport Shop (Beverly Hills)
P. 120-121 Clothes from I. Buss & Co. (New York)
P. 127 *Left*, clothes by Sal Cesarani
P. 128 *Right*, jacket & shirt by Charles Suppon
P. 129 Shirt by Bill Kaiserman for Rafael
P. 132 Jacket & tie by Egon Von Furstenberg
P. 133 Outfits by Alexander Julian
P. 135 Tuxedo by Jeffrey Banks
P. 136 *Left*, mess jacket and formal trousers by Jeffrey Banks; *right*, ensemble by Gil Truedsson for Tiger of Sweden
P. 137 Suit and vest by Gil Truedsson
P. 138 Formalwear by Sal Cesarani
P. 140 *Left*, clothes by Bill Blass
P. 141 *Top*, styled by Alan Flusser
P. 145 Clothes by Jeffrey Banks
P. 146-147 Suit by Bill Blass; *146*, shirt by Bill Blass, sweater by Robert Stock for Country Roads, tie by Bert Pulitzer; *147*, shirt & tie by Bert Pulitzer, vest by Hickey-Freeman
P. 149 Clothes by Bill Kaiserman for Rafael; worn by Douglas Hess
P. 151 Clothes worn by Christopher Petkanas
P. 152 Clothes worn by Ray Underwood
P. 155-156 Clothes worn by Tom Fallon
P. 157-159 Clothes worn by Conrad Bell
P. 160 Clothes by Ronald Kolodzie
P. 161 Clothes worn by Bob Dahlin
P. 163 Clothes worn by Ron Wegen
P. 164 Headgear by Marsha Akins for Makins Hats
P. 165 *Top left*, suit jacket by Oscar de La Renta

P. 167 *Top right*, clothes by Ronald Kolodzie; *left*, Lee Wright for G.B. Pedrini; *lower right*, shirt by Charles Suppon, belts by Nancy Knox Ltd.
P. 171 *Lower right*, clothes by Bill Kaiserman for Rafael
P. 173 Clothes by Bill Kaiserman
P. 175 Sport jacket by Graham & Gunn, Ltd.
P. 179 Sweater by Nancy Knox Ltd.
P. 181 Clothes from Maxfield Bleu (Beverly Hills)
P. 196 *Top*, suit by Sal Cesarani; *bottom*, suit by Jeffrey Banks
P. 197 *Left*, suit & shirt by Bill Kaiserman for Rafael; *top right*, jacket & pants from Country Britches; *lower right*, clothes & cap by Gil Truedsson for Tiger of Sweden.
P. 198 *Left*, jacket & pants from Country Britches, shirt & tie by Bert Pulitzer; *top right*, styled by Sal Cesarani; *lower right*, jacket & pants from Country Britches.
P. 199 Clothes by Lee Wright for San Remo
P. 200 *Left*, suit by Pierre Cardin, tie by Vicky Davis
P. 201 *Top left*, shirt by Robert Stock for Country Roads; *lower left & right*, clothes by Bill Blass
P. 203 *Right*, shirt by Robert Stock for Country Roads
P. 204 Pants by T.T. Gurtner
P. 206 *Left*, sportswear by Sal Cesarani
P. 207 Clothes by Lee Wright for G.B. Pedrini
P. 210 Styled by Lee Wright
P. 211 Coat by Petkanas Bros.
P. 212 *Right*, coat by Lee Wright for San Remo
P. 213 *Right*, coat by Bill Kaiserman for Rafael
P. 214 Coat by Pierre Cardin Relax
P. 217-219 Suit by Pierre Cardin; *218*, sweat pants by Alan Flusser; *219, top*, jacket by David Shapiro; *bottom*, jacket from Pierre Cardin Relax, sweater from Ursel
P. 220-221 Sweater from Paul Stuart; *left*, T-shirt & pants by Ronald Kolodzie; *right*, suit by Jeffrey Banks
P. 222-223 Blazer by Jacques Esterel, Paris; *222*, slacks, vest & tie by Alexander Julian, shirt from Brooks Bros.; *223, lower right*, shirts, slacks, sweater and tie by Alexander Julian
P. 224 Jacket & slacks by Sal Cesarani
P. 232 Pants by Pierre Cardin
P. 233 *Left*, styled by Alexander Julian; *lower right*, jacket & tie by Bill Blass
P. 234 *Right*, sportswear by Ron Chereskin
P. 238 *Lower left & right*, clothes by Jeffrey Banks
P. 243 Clothes by Yves St. Laurent

INDEX